RECLAIMING
A
NATION

TRACEY LEIGH

CONTENTS

Once upon a time there was a mighty nation.

It sat just below Canada's location.

Morale was high and women were chaste,

Men were strong and children obeyed.

The poor were fed and the widows were loved,

While the populous trembled at the Word from above.

Prayer in school was a way of life,

And the President stood for more than the trite.

The pulpits were flamed and the preachers were too,

As America was once a place free to choose.

Now infanticide is cherished, and sex is the language,

Witchcraft entertainment, and Allah is sanctioned.

So the droughts have come, and the famines will too.

Storms have devastated, and more than a few.

A new era has dawned in the land of the free,

As Communism is pledged, it surely will be.

We must turn to God and finally awake,

Dropping our idols of eternal mistake!

If we pray now our mighty shores will ring,

With freedom again from Jesus the King.

INTRODUCTON

The answer for America or any nation is not political change. We will never create enough laws to solve the problems that only obeying God can fix. The solution to a spiraling nation, regardless of occupational choice is found in making Jesus, Lord. When the people of a land decide to cast away their idols of worldliness and seek God's face, then reclamation can begin. When following the Lord becomes the top priority, things will change. When those of us who know how to pray actually pray, things will change.

Warrior-heart praying *will* save a nation. History proves it! But don't be misled, this approach is different all together. It is fervent, intense, on purpose, uncompromising and powerful in delivery, producing alteration. It commits for the long haul. And it isn't appeasing, man pleasing, idolatrous or shy in nature. Those who have honed their spiritual abilities, living from a place of humility, purity and self-discipline will be the ones with a voice in this hour. These will be the individuals who will reclaim nations, cities and continents.

Possessing a voice to reclaim a nation will cost everything. It will cost us the privilege of walking in the flesh and will require we live holy lives, separating ourselves from the filth of the world. It will mean we are persecuted and rejected by friends, family and so-called Church leaders who do not understand God's ways. It will demand we actually produce reformation in prayer by keeping our minds focused, so that we are effective. Know this: America's pathway out of the pit is none other than prolonged, fervent intercession and extended periods of spontaneous worship to God, induced by the individuals explained above! I'm convinced if just one person reaches the place of brokenness where pride is crucified, we will experience revivals of unprecedented magnitude. God is waiting on *us* to obey!

THE BACKDROP

The following pages are more than a glorified journal of my personal travels. They are consecutive, true-life stories that could actually double as a modern-day archetype for revival. Every story is shared deliberately, revealing the ambiguous but obvious protocol for reclaiming a nation. So this book is not merely about *my* journey, it is about equipping those who desire to see regional awakenings, and long for practical examples. For this purpose, I have carefully penned every dream, vision, and prophetic word for the benefit of others. And every challenge and victory was recorded with the nations of the earth in mind. Although the backdrop is set in America and the clarion call came from God to the United States, these same concepts will apply to any land because they are not my ideals, but His.

Now, possessing territory for the glory of the Lord and the salvation of many will always begin in the heart of travail. Apostolic intercession *must* precede apostolic actions of which the simple, practical stories in this book are a prime illustration. So to be clear, true apostles must rise up and do their job in intercession *and* action. It requires the apostles' authority to actually change a region! They are the ones God has gifted to deal with the atmospheric strongholds, as well as the setting of leaders in place. Without the apostles we won't get very far. (And I'm not speaking about business-card apostles either. When a real apostle steps on the scene, they are extremely humble and slightly terrifying.)

Throughout this book, in city after city, the leaders with which God connected me were all apostolic. Many of them were unaware of their gifting because they had been serving in the church system. And that system does everything but encourage apostles to rise up. It only wants followers who will build egos instead of God's kingdom. This is important to say up front because of what happened when I went into the various regions. I was not there to build a personal ministry, I was following God's urgent directive to help save a nation. So my role was to awaken and serve by my every action and through my travail, while simultaneously imparting a greater ability to build. Since I, myself was moving apostolically, God was anointing me to do this, as well as displace man-made traditions and territorial principalities. One leader said to me, "You are dealing with the stuff in the atmosphere so we can mobilize the troops on the ground." This ability was given in a heavenly encounter and through His commissioning at the beginning.

The apostolic arrangement I'm describing is just the beginning of the proper alignment that must occur in order for God's government to operate upon the earth. It is *His* government moving through *His* people in a heavenly order that will transform the hurting countries of the world.

TIME LINE

The following story begins in the fall of 2012.
It ends, November 2013.

1

THE CALL

It was a beautiful fall morning. The streets were empty and I was driving through the city watching the sun pour over the horizon. My coffee was smooth and piping hot. Then suddenly, the bold voice of the Lord entered my atmosphere.

"A prayer initiative to turn a nation. A strategy to awaken a nation that has gone dry."

He continued, "But it's not really dry."

I quickly pulled my SUV into the nearest lot and came to a screeching halt! Tangible glory filled my vehicle, as I rummaged frantically through my door panels searching for paper. I found several pages of a stapled together document and hurriedly turned it over to the blank backsides. The heavenly monologue continued, while my spirit was simultaneously lifted above America.

"There are wells beneath the ground that must be re-awakened and tapped."

I looked and saw huge pools of water just beneath the surface of many cites. They were blue and vibrant, gigantic in size, even spanning entire towns. My gaze focused toward the northeastern part of America.

The Lord continued, "Holiness is a part of this land, it is a heritage for this people. You will call them back to their purpose and re-establish or re-put the vision before them, the American people. There will be a response far and wide, as many will be saved and restored. The great revival that has been prophesied is about to manifest. People are ready and they are hungry."

I called to mind the revivals of repentance that had graced our shores throughout the centuries. None of them had originated from politics, or masses voting for better laws. Each time it was a people turning wholeheartedly to the Lord. This is an important fact, because this fall morning fell eight weeks before America's presidential election. And the Christians' obsession with candidates so blinded them; they couldn't see God's strategy for turning a nation. This revival would not come through voting in a righteous Politian! And it was evident through the view unfolding before me, the scene was nothing less than a passion gripping multitudes to know a holy God.

His words continued furiously, "You were called, purposed and born to awaken a nation. Go like fire! Plow a path. Leave a trail. Plow over anything that stands in your way. Don't stop. Keep moving! You will form the truest, purest path; free of idolatry, judgment and worship of man. This is why I have chosen you, because of your heart. It is free from idolatry and desire for attention and position. In your heart it is truly not about you but about Me and glorifying Me.

Shake off the past season of mockery for I will bring all things together. I will establish you. Don't give up on the passion for your nation! See it, and hold on to it. Don't let it go, with all of your might! Hang on to it and declare it; trumpet it! Awaken a nation. Awaken a generation. I will send you to gateway cities and gate cites to prophesy and to raise up – to turn a nation. There is nothing like what you are about to do and what you will be a part of. Stay true. Awaken yourself. For you will be the trumpet to sound. Tell America to stop pushing the snooze button!"

The next phase of this vision for America consisted of worshiping musicians. I knew my past involvement with a worship movement had been the first layer of strategy. These fiery musicians would churn a harvest of souls and usher God back into America. I had to re-enter this realm of mobilizing corporate worship and prayer.

The command progressed, "Worshipers and intercessors are the rudder for the nation. It is not politicians that will turn America. Worshipers and intercessors are going to create the atmosphere conducive for climatic change in cities of America. Without them change will not occur! They control the waves, what they say goes. Hold worship meetings and only worship. Hold prayer meetings and only pray. Pray in the prayer meetings and worship in the worship meetings- no other agenda. Pray or worship. That's it! The initiative is to gather the musicians and intercessors for an all-out onslaught of glory in the Spirit."

At this point, I watched a deluge of golden rain pound the ground from above. It looked like Niagara Falls falling on cities. This barrage was coming from intercessors releasing power through heavenly tongues. It was also coming from musicians as they released frequencies of praise to cleanse the atmosphere. The key was bombardment! Bombarding the nation with the glory of God and refusing to back down would change everything. I knew it! It was so clear to me. No one, or nothing, could stand a chance if God's glory was released at concentrated levels.

The Lord continued, "This mandate is the sword I gave you in Nebraska. Use it. Wield it. Pack your stuff and go! Prepare to go. Prepare for flight. I will give you such influence and a voice; use it wisely. For the sword is very, very sharp and has the ability to cut down quickly, words and agendas that are not of Me. Only cut down what I want cut down. You are a very unusual warrior. Make no apologies for who you are, for I will give you favor. Your uniqueness will also give you favor with the world and worldly people." I recalled my encounter with God six days prior, as well as the consecutive five days. They had been a mystery, until this moment!

THE SWORD AND NEBRASKA

I had driven to Nebraska for a mini-vacation; half a week to be exact. It was a sunny afternoon and the day before my 39th birthday. My spirit was oddly agitated. As evening drew near, I retreated and set my Mac to repeat a worship song innumerably. The air around me electrified and was most enchanting. It was like a heavenly, fairy tale. I tried to pray but couldn't. I tried to sing, it fell flat. So I knelt beside my bed, folding my hands together and resting my forehead on my fingers.

When I closed my eyes my spirit was transported before the Lord, My Lover. In His throne room I appeared. It was bronze and mildly glowing with fire. He was seated. And from a little distance I knelt down and began to weep. I tried to pray in tongues once again, but to no avail. So I gave way to the Lord and remained quietly before Him. Something was happening and it was very intimate. He was communicating His love and jealously for me. He adored me deeply and His acceptance was undeniable. This moment last for many moments.

After a bit of time, I was suddenly aware of the silver band on the ring finger of my right hand. I knew it was to be transferred to my left one, my wedding finger. So through the weeping and shaky arms, I made the switch. The emotion of His love for me intensified. It was like a ceremony. Now my sobs were so deep I felt I was being turned inside out. I knew I was His. I belonged to Him. The Lord, Himself was betrothing me; taking me as His own, as unfathomable billows of love rolled from Him toward me. This proceeded for quite some time, and still, I could not sing or pray.

Eventually, I pulled myself up to sit on the bed, crossed-legged, head in hands and weeping. This lasted too, until I was completely overcome by the Presence of God. Eventually, I raised my head and opened my eyes. Before my face was a sword suspended

4

laterally! I peered beyond the blade through the Spirit into my future. A narrow, curvy pathway came into view.

The Lord spoke, "I am giving you this sword early. It was designed for your forties but you will receive it now so you can learn to wield it."

I was aghast, but did the obvious and grabbed the steely weapon. Authority to decree and set my forthcoming era came strongly upon me! I began hurling Spirit-born phrases, while shocks of power jolted my body. This dominion was unmistakable and effortless. Something had altered while I was in the throne-room, I felt tangibly different. My emotions were settled, sound and secure, as confidence and healing, replaced rejection and betrayals. This was odd because I had no control over what was happening. I had not been petitioning Him. It was a sovereign transition; He picked me up from one realm and transferred me into another.

The decrees continued and so did the bolts of power. I could feel boldness to live the impossible settling upon me. I saw who I was in the Spirit and it was frightening! The fear of the Lord would now be my companion. And this terrifying Presence would not be reckoned with or stopped. It would forever be a mainstay in my future.

RIGHTEOUSNESS PREVAILS

I scanned the room and the clock revealed a fast approaching midnight. My body was weary from the car drive and long hours at my retail job. I decided to lie down and sleep, my Mac still on repeat. As my side hit the mattress I took a deep breath and relaxed. But no sooner had I exhaled, than another jolt of power hit me. The force compelled me upright and a shouting roar came out of my mouth. Suddenly, I was in another vision!

I watched as the space in front of me was blanketed with the power sounding from my mouth. In that area stood many mockers of the gospel, both heathens and supposed Christians. They appeared like columns standing in their own doctrines made of whom they created God to be. But His righteousness was disintegrating them and they were quickly becoming dust in the wind.

This virtue was coming from my mouth, while my spirit emanated, "No! That's not right! That's not true! This is truth!"

These mockers could not endure the frequency of Truth riding on my voice. (This moment was extremely intense and I maintained no control over what was happening, including the visions I was seeing.) After this I laid back down, puzzled. Why did I have no province over myself? Then all of a sudden, another wave hit! A long and powerful sound roared out, as a force from the Lord hurled me up. This was followed by another vision. This time it slightly altered from the previous one, as before me stood the vilest, human souls perpetrating their filth. Once more, the righteousness from my mouth consumed them in an instant. All forsook the ability to stand. A very pure indignation was flowing out of me and it appeared nothing could stop it!

This process continued a few more times. Each vision slightly varied but all were related to those who had built their lives on deception. Finally, I was able to fall asleep. As the night progressed I woke frequently, as jolts of power riveted my body. After this, I rested a day and a half, and then returned to Oklahoma. The electric shocks continued on the long drive. (As a matter of fact, they continued for many days).

THE 5 A.M. PRAYER

TWO DAYS LATER: It was Wednesday, and two days after my return. 4:30 a.m. typically comes early but I awoke unusually energetic. I called to mind an early prayer gathering that started at 5 a.m. I arrived just in time for the ending. My friends surrounded me and began to pray as they saw me enter the room. I felt great heat upon my body and confirmation of their spoken words. From there I was invited to an impromptu prayer session that would take place in a few hours.

THE AWAKENING

TWO HOURS LATER: When I arrived at the unplanned meeting. I sat Indian-style on the floor with my face down. Suddenly, I felt the hand of a prophet on the top of my head!

She began to prophesy many things about my future, "For there is a blue-printing plan ahead. Do not be man-led but Spirit-led and I will raise you up and you will see I have filled your cup with a fresh anointing…And My glory and My truth in an hour of shaking will come to you. And the awakening, the awakening, you will herald it like a trumpet, with a Spirit upon you that only I can give. Seek Me as you've never done before, for you stand at My very door. Now, ask and seek and knock, for it is opened unto you, and I will bring you up into the heavenlies. And you will see the plan that I have for you, and for this people, and for this hour, for this nation."

I was completely baffled and knew my time in Oklahoma was short.

DRAFTED

As I sat in the parking lot that Thursday morning, writing and reminiscing, one hundred and twenty minutes had passed. Now it all made sense, the sword, the commissioning, and the supernatural stability. God needed me, and He needed me now, to drop everything and GO. I felt as if I had received draft papers in the mail and was given two weeks to say goodbye. I was a modern-day Jonah being thrown upon the shores of Nineveh! For months I had been ignoring God's promptings, even heading in the opposite direction. But I could not escape the mantle He placed upon me.

REFORMER'S ANOINTING OIL

Now, I was scheduled to meet a very important friend for a car trip downtown. So I hurriedly collected myself and went to meet her. I was still processing the previous two hours when I jumped into her car. As soon as I shut the door she said, "Tracey get your phone, record this. I have a word for you. I never do this but I think you should record it."

So, I raised my phone and pressed the button. She wasted no time speaking in a quiet voice, as we started down riverside drive.

"God has a special gift for you for your birthday. It is the reformer's anointing oil. Evidently, it has been reserved in heaven for quite sometime and it's only for certain generations and only certain people can have it. I'm not sure if it's actual oil, or if it is an anointing, but the Lord wants you to have it. You are going to anoint people with it and you'll be surprised whom The Lord will have you anoint. This reformer's anointing oil is going to be like the Arab Spring. It is going to unite the generations, young and old. Even the media will report it."

She went on to talk about the price I had paid and wept through her tears, as she continued to speak words from the Lord to me. Our car ride was over too soon and I was left pondering another perplexing word spoken over my life.

THE COST

On Saturday, I was taking a lovely drive down a back road and enjoying the many fall colors. My mind was rambling along. I was by myself and didn't like it. My next birthday would turn me 40 and the lack of a godly, male counterpart overwhelmed me. But no matter how hard I tried, each time I was left alone. Out of frustration, I began pouring out my heart to God when He interrupted my agenda,

"Will you not get married?" He showed me a strict time period. "Can you sacrifice your desires and what you want and go to the cities I will send you?"

The words hit like an arrow! Then ease, and I began to cry. He continued, "I gave My life for you. Can you give Me your life? I died for you. I'm asking for your life in return. Will you give up your personal comforts for one year and go to where I will send you? I gave My life for you, will you give your life for Me?" I cried and cried as I drove through those beautiful, narrow roads.

The Lord revealed more, "You are going to be alone. It's called sacrifice. Reformers are alone. Some lives are created for other people. You were born for other people."

He just kept repeating the cost of sacrifice. How could I say no to a God who ransomed me? Not only did He deliver me from eternal hell, but also He pulled me out of a miry pit orchestrated for my destruction. That rescue came back to my remembrance. It was years ago when He allowed my escape from an oppressive, nuptial agreement. I had said to Him at the time, "My life would have been nothing had You not heard my cry and delivered me from the bondage. Now, I am forever indebted to You, My God. Take my life and do with it as You will."

That memory hit hard! I could not argue with God. Besides, He gave me grace during our conversation. So through my tears I whispered, "Yes, God I will go. I will go wherever You send me, and not get married for a while. I will sacrifice my personal comforts and desires."

I felt a release. I returned to my retail job announcing my two-week notice. To my surprise the managers knew, the Lord had told them! So where, and when were the remaining mysteries. The next week would prove to be nothing short of a miraculous re-ordering of my life.

THE RECLUSE

The day after saying yes to God I detected a bump under the skin on the back of my thigh. It quickly grew in diameter, as well as in depth. Within a few days the pain was so intense I could barely lift my leg to walk. The skin was turning black and I discovered I had been bitten by a brown recluse spider! The poison in my system made me extremely nauseous, and it lasted for five days. My faith was challenged because I could not take antibiotics; hence, I had to trust God that I would not lose a huge piece of flesh. Resting for recovery was impossible, as my work hours increased, causing me to stand for grueling segments of time. At night I could not sleep. Those hours were reserved for propping up my body to air out infected skin, because it was bandaged all day at work. The rest of my time was spent downsizing my belongings, packing for a one-year trip and making phone calls. I had to move fast to figure out my schedule, my timeline to leave was short!

After treating the bite with charcoal for a few days, the infection was curbed, and a small portion of tissue fell off. The black skin may have been gone, but I was left with extreme exhaustion. The sickness, lack of sleep, and intense work hours, mixed with the stress of not knowing my future was unreal. Nevertheless I had to persevere, the unknown road awaited me.

Next, a very crucial phone call was made to my revivalist friend in Ohio. For seven months I had ignored God's promptings, but finally I obeyed and contacted him. When he heard my commissioning and the Lord's words he suggested I come to Ohio. It was just as the Lord showed me! Next I called my former college pastor and relayed the mandate.

His response, "Tracey I was just now reading in the book of Acts about the apostles when they laid their hands on people and sent them out."

I asked, "So you're saying I need to have a group of leaders lay hands on me and send me out?"

He said, "No. I'm saying *you* need to lay hands on people."

I was silent. "It's time." He said.

Then, Arkansas opened up. God secured a place for me to share the message there. This would be my first stop on the way to Ohio. So after many long retail hours, the spider bite, and the scheduling of a new life, I trashed half of my belongings, and shoved the rest in a closet that was not my own.

2

THE PATH

As I rolled into Little Rock, Arkansas I felt extreme joy. It was here that I had experienced the greatest of times. The trees, the peace, the hills, the terrain, and oh, the humble people! Even though I had been here often, clocking countless hours in intercession, I never noticed the "ark" in the state's name. It seemed to be glowing as I whizzed by the road sign.

Immediately, the Lord began a conversation about the Ark of the Covenant and its important symbolism. The Presence of God was the foundation of my mission and America's pathway out of the pit. The bottom-line: without His Presence we are nothing and have nothing. Our Christian labor and benevolence is in vain without Him. (I soon learned my unknown path was His timely articulation for America.)

REVIVAL HERITAGE

The church God connected me with in Arkansas had experienced an extensive revival, many moons ago. I was told the Pastor was well-known for this. He and his wife were amazing people, possessing the purest of hearts. And I'm pretty sure he was a prophet! (He gave me three concrete words that came to pass very quickly.) I spoke at this church on two different Sunday mornings. One of them stands out. I began the message with a 5-minute video about Navy SEALs. It showed how well-equipped they were for battle, as they rescued a hostage with exact precision in mere minutes. It was quite riveting. We must live like the SEALs, spiritually; all of our gifts honed to perfection. We must be ready in record-time to deliver a people or a nation.

I gave the message for America and then called the congregation to the front. It flooded with people. Next I induced a warrior-heart anointing by taking a set of congas. Thankfully, three drummers came to my rescue, while I took to the altar. I laid hands on everyone's forehead, as I prayed in tongues over the microphone. Soon, I was singing songs of authority and power along with the drumming percussionists. They must have played for over an hour! The service lasted until 2 p.m. About this time, I went to the parking lot and was met by a man who informed me he *never* stays after church. He was lit up, and let me know how miraculous it was that he was still present.

While I was here I held a small prayer school at the host church. And there was a lot of impartation for sure! But the following week was a little rocky for me, I couldn't seem to land a date in Toledo. My revivalist friend was having challenges with his schedule. I began to wonder if it was ever going to happen and grew quite discouraged. (God had sent me on a one-year mission and this was only the second week. And I couldn't even secure the second city! To make emotional matters worse, a strong intercessor said she had a word for me,

"Go back home. You have some family issues that need healing."

Was she serious? My home-town family was lovely, we had no problems whatsoever. Needless to say, I wrestled with this false word for a couple of weeks, hoping Toledo would hurry up and open, because I had no third city either! (If Ohio fell through, I was bust.) Finally, I concluded the erroneous word must have been a test to see if I was going to follow the Lord, or a strong intercessor. I'm glad I chose Jesus.

A STEP OVER THE RIVER

While I was in Little Rock I spent time with a powerful sister in the Lord. She shared a story with me that I can't help but think relates to all of this. God had given her an assignment to drive to Colorado and climb to the place where the Arkansas River began. Her instructions: pour anointing oil in it; believe for revival. She and her family made the long trek and found the spot; she stepped over the start of a river and initiated a movement of God. This is one of those hidden things people do in obedience to the Lord and the repercussions are immeasurable!

THE DREAM

Also while in Arkansas, I had a significant dream.

I dreamt I was in Tulsa, suspended about one thousand feet in the atmosphere. I was looking down upon the city and saw the foundation of a church. Nothing remained but a concrete slab. The pastors and congregants were standing upon the spot that had once sported their sanctuary. I cried from the air, offering an opportunity to receive revival.

A grimacing face and a shaking forefinger was the congenial response, "No! We don't want it!" the pastor cried back.

Instantly, my eyes scanned the city looking for someone else to say yes. I began to weep. My sight then landed on another influential church. That one too, said no to a mighty move of God. My weeping turned into wails at their rejection of the Lord.

Then suddenly the scene changed. The entire planet was small before me and I was shown the top half of the earth's curvature. As I stared, a few intercessors materialized, standing shoulder to shoulder. They joined hands and began to pray. Then more emerged next to them they too, held hands. I watched a line of intercessors form across the top portion of the globe. But it wasn't just a single-file line, the rows quickly multiplied in depth as well.

This process repeated itself, until an indefinite amount of people joined the ranks. Many stepped forward from all nations and walks of life. There was no end to the procession that was forming. Then, the innumerable collection of souls looked up, lifted their hands and cried out in prayer. What happened next was profound. The huge, profile face of God appeared, it was almost the size of the entire globe! He was so close; His nose nearly grazed them. He was looking upon them and smiling big. It seemed the whole world was gathered on the circle of the earth, lifting their voices and faces to God. The glory was thick across the ground's surface, as man and God united.

This dream revealed an intimate detail of my past and would encourage me in the near future. I had been rejected in Tulsa because of my style of intercession and pursuit for revival, but God was using me anyway. He was about to birth an awakening far greater than one city, and it would not be stopped! When leaders of renown reject those God has chosen, His plan still cannot be averted.

THE CRAZY LADY

After two weeks in Arkansas, I drove to Hot Springs to attend a powerful meeting, hoping the impartation would fill my spirit. This would be my last night before driving to Ohio. I was excited and sat near the back. But my glee was cut short by a squirrely lady intercessor that mistook me for a witch!

She stood about two feet away and faced me. With her back to the stage, she spoke the blood of Jesus and quoted scriptures over and over. I leaned to the side so I could see the preacher, but she did too, blocking my view. So I scooted several seats down and tried to ignore Ms. Squirrely's preposterous activity. But she scurried sideways and stood in front of me, still quoting. I changed rows several more times until eventually, I was at the other side of the

14

sanctuary. She followed me each and every time, frantically pacing. I couldn't focus at all, so I left. Consequently, I was spiritually and physically fatigued from all of her negative vigor. Oh, how true discernment is needed in the body of Christ. Intercessors must be trained properly! (I suspected my black stiletto boots and matching shirt was the basis for her flakiness.)

TOLEDO, OHIO

12 HOURS LATER: I left Arkansas and drove fourteen more to Toledo. I arrived at 2:30 a.m. Needless to say I was exhausted and still dealing with the repercussions of the spider bite. I was shown to my sleeping quarters which was the renovated, third floor of an old Masonic temple. The heat in the building was shut off so it was very cold for this Oklahoma girl. (And sadly, the electric heater on the floor by the couch evaded detection.)

I managed to sleep three hours amid rattling doors in the large, empty edifice. At first I thought it was homeless people in the area trying to get inside, but soon I realized it was only evil spirits. I guess the structure didn't like me much. I arose at 6 a.m. to a very cold loft with a craving for something hot. My sleeping bag didn't do much for the frigid air that had seeped through the cracks in the old windows. But at least I didn't have to sleep in my car, which I was willing to do in order to obey God's desperate plea for America.

After rummaging around the city I found a good coffee shop. This soothed my soul. But I remained slightly comatose, saying to myself I was too old for this. I wanted to be enjoying life with a man of God. But not so! I was here in Toledo with no inkling of my next location, only that I would be on the road for a year. Forcefully, I put that out of my mind and waited for my revivalist friend to call.

He contacted me early evening and we sat down face to face. It wasn't such a smooth conversation, either. God had shown me many things would occur in the cities and with the people in which I was aligning. I tried to explain some of these mysteries but in the end they remained just that, mysteries! As we talked, he informed me I would be speaking that night (in a few hours). I had no message and I was exhausted but I had no choice, so I trusted God. Originally, I was scheduled for the following week, I was hoping to use the spare time to rest and recover a bit. Also I wanted to explore and discern the land, which would help me hear what the Lord was saying for Toledo. Obviously the Lord had a different plan.

Soon, we ended our coffee chat and he gave me directions to where I could shower. I had forty-five minutes to find the home, clean up and drive to the service. Amazingly, I did it! In the rush of the moment, I grabbed the nearest, cleanest clothes in the back of my SUV. So, I entered the sanctuary with random apparel, sopping wet hair and a face that bore only a smidgen of three-day old eyeliner. I went to the back where the leaders prayed beforehand.

After a few minutes, they finished and walked by me single-file, right out of the little room. My revivalist friend acknowledged me with a quick pat on the shoulder, as he was the last to pass by. I followed the trail into the congregation and the service began. It was like electricity in the atmosphere! The musicians were incredible. These passionate ones, mixed with the presence of my fiery friend made me all the more nervous. You see, I was not an experienced speaker, and if ever I attended a church, I always preferred the back row. And of course, multiplying my relaxed feeling was my dripping wet hair in the heat-deprived building! So there I stood, in the dimly lit congregation singing along, wondering what to say when handed the microphone. Finally, I sat down, exasperated.

The Lord then spoke, "Toledo is to be a windbreak to prevent the Spirit of Islam from sweeping over the rest of the nation."

My first thought, "What's a windbreak?" I quickly googled it on my phone, as God unpacked the most simple strategy for this great spiritual military city! They were to praise the Lord relentlessly and pray ferociously, thereby throwing up an invisible barrier that would squelch the spread of Islam. These warriors were called to displace darkness with their worship. I delivered the message in a rather meek, inexperienced tone, but the Lord was in it.

Afterwards, a worship leader from another congregation approached me, "You're not staying in this building another night!" I was so thankful I almost cried. His benevolent church picked up the bill, as my millions were going fast.

When my refreshing night in solitude ended, I stayed at a host home. It was nice, but it came with certain restraints. These included schedules arranged to make it tough for me to shower daily, and some late nights waiting in my car. Since I was not given a key, there were times I could not return until the owner was home, which meant I sat in my vehicle, waiting. I didn't have the money to let my car idle. Not a big deal, but when it's winter in the northeast, it's very cold! The schedule was so manipulated that at the end of my tenure I took a shower at another house. (Again, I reminded myself God had asked me to give up my comforts.)

I remained in the city for a few weeks, greeting new faces and leaders. The most amazing ones were some apostolic pastors who were mobilizing the city. The wife invited me to Thanksgiving dinner upon my first introduction to her. The people in their church turned out to be some of the best friends to me. Initially, when I arrived, I knew only my revivalist friend, but that was quickly changing. Most of those I met were accommodating and excited to hear of my commission. But one was a bit opposing.

In the first small meeting with leaders, I was challenged by a local Pastor who expressed he didn't need me and could pray himself. He asked who was I that pastors in his city should budget for my spiritual labor. I wasn't asking for money, I was on assignment from the Lord to simply convey the message to intercessors. His words brought confusion but I determined to keep calm and follow the Lord. (Challenges always preceded great opportunities!) Later that week, my revivalist friend opened his building and I organized a prayer school and a few meetings. During those fourteen days, I grew in anxiety because my next location was not yet secured. But I kept in contact with a friend from New York who had helped me through many trials. He knew of my journey and seemed supportive, but was probably watching to see the outcome of my crazy shenanigan. Then, I received an email from him about a pastor who wanted to talk to me. Her church was in western New York. She invited me to hold a prayer school in her city. I accepted.

In the course of the conversation, she mentioned she would be recording a TV program on the morning after my arrival. And it would be good for me to see the studio, just not on that day. But the Lord whispered in my ear to go anyway. So I left Toledo a few days earlier than I planned and started the trek to New York.

THE FINNEY PIECE

I was just east of Toledo when I spotted a green, road sign. The city name grabbed my attention. It was familiar and I exited immediately. Someone told me year's prior that Charles Finney was buried in Ohio. I discovered it was true and his graveside was a mere 20 miles away. This was one field trip I was not going to miss!

On the back roads to the cemetery, the sun was setting and the snow was bright. I was thinking about some of the stories of his life. The most intriguing was one of a commercial business he visited. He entered the building and without speaking a word, the entire place ended up in a state of repentance until the whole group was born-again. The man's intensity had gripped me, as well as his walk of holiness and fire. I didn't know much about him and thought he lived and preached mostly in England, but I was about to discover otherwise!

I arrived at a gigantic cemetery. In my zeal, I failed to realize I did not know the man, so consequently I had no idea where he was buried. Instinctively though, I drove to a back corner. I sat there a little befuddled. How could I possibly find the head stone amid hundreds of others? I looked at the picture I found on the Internet, and knew I was in the right vicinity, but still it was too vast.

The Lord spoke, "Get out and walk."

So I did. I walked about thirty feet from my SUV and there was his headstone, slightly taller than myself. I stood reading it and thinking, now what? Aha! Take a picture. I kept cutting out the words and had to retake it several times, which caused me to stand on the ground for quite a while. The sunset was peeping over my head, making my hair look like fire shooting off of my face. Quite fascinating. It was nice, but very cold and high time to head into New York!

I left the cemetery and started for the highway. After ten minutes had passed I felt something on the bottoms of my feet. At first I thought I had stepped in something, so I looked around my petals, but saw nothing. Then I thought it must be my car heater so I moved my feet around trying to figure out the source. Suddenly, energy shot up my body! It felt as if I could run 90 miles.

"What is this?" I began to pray.

The grave! I stood on that thing forever. Then I remembered the biblical story of Elisha. His bones retained tangible power while his body lay in the ground.

I thought, "No way. That guy has been dead a long time."

At any rate, I was now caught in intercession for America. Over and over, I wept and sang for my country to cry out for the cleansing blood of Jesus. After a few hours, I asked the Lord for the word to uncap the well of the next city. But as I drove through the dark, wintry night I heard nothing. Howbeit, in the Spirit, I saw a huge lion head roaring out of the mountains of New York.

The Lord said, "That is the state of New York."

Hmm. Rather interesting. All of a sudden, I found myself driving in increasing amounts of snowfall. I had been traveling through the rural countryside and now mountains, for miles. It was getting harder and harder to see. The view through my windshield was like traveling through outer space. (I was told I was in a blizzard!) Suddenly, I was descending a huge hill, nothing but a steep drop to my right. I was scared and pumping my breaks. The car's speed was increasing, and increasing fast. I was praying fervently not to slide off of the road. Finally, I reached the bottom. My phone rang. It was my New York friend who had helped me though many trials.

"Watch the hill on such and such road!" He said.

Oh, that hill. Nice timing. Either way, I was nearing the very rural region of my host home as my G.P.S. took me straight to the street. But something was wrong. It wasn't her home! So I called her.

She said, "Wrong city."

Then she rattled off, go this way, and that way. I was now turning down all the correct roads, until I neared the vicinity of her house. Suddenly I lost signal on my phone and G.P.S. I fought off panic as I saw nothing but vast expanses of snow and rustic back roads. It was dark and I was lost, and I was so, so tired. But somehow my mind remembered what she recited right before the call dropped. By the grace of God, I arrived at her home at 10 p.m. She immediately showed me to my room.

I was worn out from the drive, the snow, the stress, the intercession and the warfare from Toledo. So I was anxious to fall asleep but I could not; I was restless. I was drawn to the picture of myself at Finney's headstone. I kept looking at it. All night long I tossed around, clicking my phone off and on glaring at the sight. Why was I so intrigued? Finally I arose from bed, heavy with spiritual agitation. I needed to steal away with God to release some intercession; I could feel it sitting on me.

As I climbed the stairs to sneak out and pray, the pastor grabbed me, "Come up here for tea and a muffin."

So I joined her in the kitchen. I figured I needed to eat anyway, but very quickly, as the Lord was pressing me. After two hours of sitting at the table listening to stories, I could hold back no longer. I opened my mouth to tell what God was saying over America, but I was swept up in a burst of tears and travailing prayer. I quickly grabbed some napkins and tried to collect myself. I struggled to stop weeping. I took another bite of muffin and sipped some tea, to appear normal. But the heaves and sobs came back even harder. I was soon doubled-over in my seat wailing for revival. Twenty minutes had passed when the pastor looked at me from across the table, "You've got to birth it."

Then power from heaven hit my body. I sat erect, and began a discourse in heavenly tongues with an accent and authority I had not known.

"Bear down, God!" I shouted, "Bear down on the land!"

I began to prophesy and wondered at the strange drawl that I was hearing, as my words in English flowed like rivers. Also, I questioned the phrase "bear down" and its meaning. I had never heard it before, but I knew in my spirit it had something to do with Charles Finney. There was some sort of connection to what God did through His day and what was about to happen in mine. While I was prophesying, the pastor began to pace behind my chair, she was praying in tongues fervently. We did this for about an hour. Then everything became ordinary. But I felt the lightweight substance that had been resting on the surface of my skin sink into my being. It was the residue of revival from Finney's day.

After the fiery time of prayer at the kitchen table, the pastor had a short time to make it to the studio for her taping. Again, we discussed I should probably visit another time because the producer would be too busy to meet with me. (But I remembered the whisper!)

THE TV STUDIO

I arrived at the studio around lunchtime. As I walked into the break area another pastor remembered me from 2009. While we talked, the producer walked into the room and introduced himself. He asked why I was in New York. I told him about the awakening in America and God's commission to uncap the wells. He said, "I would like to have you on the program. I'm interested because you have a national vision and we are starting a new segment for topics that reach beyond the New York region." So we set the date! What favor. I was told it would air three times nationally and twice internationally.

3

WESTERN NEW YORK
AND
PENNYSLVANIA

NEW YORK'S FIRST PRAYER SCHOOL

It was Friday evening, one week after the studio introduction and
time for my first prayer school in New York. It went well, but I
was still coming out of my shell. Nevertheless, God moved. I
finished teaching on Saturday afternoon and spoke at the host
church that same night. A woman in the congregation drove from
Pennsylvania to attend this regional gathering. A man who came
on Friday invited her. When I greeted her on the way out, we
seemed to click. So we exchanged numbers and decided to have
lunch the following week.

As the morning arrived to meet her, I drove through the snowy,
rural roads of New York to get to Pennsylvania. When I neared the
border and proceeded through the mountains, I was struck with a
tightness in my chest. Fear gripped me. It felt like the oxygen had
been sucked right out of the air. I remained calm but the evil spirits
in the vicinity knew I was there. Finally, I reached the restaurant a
little light-headed.

When I sat down at the table, this woman shared the most profound miracles and moves of the Holy Spirit. All the experiences were her own! I was blown away. She was an influential woman and had revival oozing out of her pores. But, she was downcast. You see the spiritual state around her was like a desert, and she was encouraged by what I had shared at the meeting days before. It brought her hope knowing someone else was on her wavelength. She seemed like a big sister and I loved her instantly!

At the end of our lunch we decided to schedule a prayer school in her region. So after a few follow-up conversations, the date was set for mid-February in Bradford, Pennsylvania (two months away).

NEW YORK'S SECOND PRAYER SCHOOL

7 DAYS LATER: It was the week before Christmas and some intercessors scheduled a prayer school at a church in Buffalo. Since it was last minute, only a few came. I didn't mind, as God led Israel out of Egypt through one man's obedience. So we did the school, sort of. When I began to teach the questions started rolling. And my desire to answer their inquiries prevented me from sharing the much needed foundations of intercession. A lesson learned.

Shortly after the school, we organized a prayer meeting on a Monday, back at the same church. And the leader shared a picture the Lord showed her of men and women coming together to go to war. Everyone had something in common. For instance, some had a big blue cross draped over their horses, like in the crusades, while others carried a white flag with the blue cross on it. That night breakthrough came for western New York. The spiritual resistance in the atmosphere was removed. Today they are standing strong in Holy Spirit unity. They are emerging into more of what God has for the region.

In February of 2015, the prayer leader in Buffalo reminded me of that Monday evening. (She was the one who saw the picture.) She said, "Tracey, you prayed a powerful prayer that night, chasing out of the region, the demonic forces of witchcraft and disunity, among the churches and pastors. Looking back, that moment broke something in the atmosphere/region. I say that, because of the fruit I am reaping today. So, from then, until now, prayer meetings in the region have gone to a new level."

THE FLOODGATES

Immediately following this prayer school, I went to Tennessee with a friend and his family for Christmas. Along the way we stopped by the Noah's ark replica in Kentucky. It was interesting, but I still had no idea God was speaking through my pathway. As we arrived in Tennessee the laughs were great and the family amazing. But something unusual happened to me the night before we went back up north.

It was 12:45 a.m. on December 31st. I was awakened abruptly by the sound of my own voice screaming in terror. My eyes flung wide open and I was acutely alert. I had been asleep an hour and fifteen minutes, but I had had a double, night vision. It was horrifying. In this experience, it was nighttime and I was suspended above the northeast of America. Beneath me I could see the entire country sleeping, tucked tight in their beds. I looked up from my suspended position and saw three bronze-colored, horizontal floodgates. They were wide open and very large. I shouted three times, announcing,

"The floodgates are open! The floodgates are open! The floodgates are open!"

Then, I perceived their future. A muddy floodwater was about to pour through them onto the land of America, and the torrent would contain the vilest evils known to man! Then, interrupting my revelatory processing, a Caucasian Christian male appeared behind me, "Are the floodgates good?" He asked this because of the book of Malachi.

I said, "No. They're evil!"

God had opened the gates and there was nothing I could do to shut them. I screamed loudly three times, horrified! I awoke only to realize, I wasn't really awake but still dreaming. So the second vision proceeded identical to the first. But this time at the end of second one is when I screamed and woke up in real life.

I quickly calmed myself and realized the encounter was from God. So I lay very still in the pitch dark, listening. I knew whatever I heard in this moment would be critical. A song came to mind about a threshing floor. I played it on my phone and continued to listen for what God would say. My room felt consumed with blackness, like the Dark Ages; so, so bleak. I pondered the story of Abram when he fell into a deep sleep, and darkness was all around him. He was actually sensing the future of his people in the land of bondage.

Then all of a sudden, the Spirit of God illuminated me, "Joan of Arc knew she was going to die before she died. She chose to give her life."

Then the lives of Martin Luther, Evan Roberts and Charles Finney flashed before my eyes. With the appearance of each name, I saw a solitary flicker in a pitch-black setting.

"They were a single flame in the darkest times of their generation. Each saw their nation and generation changed," God said. "They were a single flicker in the darkness."

I knew what He was telling me. Even though the sons of disobedience caused heinous evils to be stored up in America, I could be the flame to ignite my country with a passion for God.

He strongly exhorted me, "Preach fervently this year against the fear of man. Confront it! Pray powerfully from the pulpits, like you do when you're alone. Don't consider offending anyone, people need to be awakened to the truth."

He warned, this was a "laying down my life", because those who wanted to live in deception but call it Christianity would persecute me. I would lose friends and lukewarm believers from my life, but I had to confront the corruption and take the hits.

God ended by saying, "Noah was a preacher of righteousness. Be a preacher of righteousness."

Another puzzle piece! I was quickly reminded of the series of dreams I had had over the previous two weeks. In all three dreams the common denominators were: muddy floodwater and animals. Their interpretation was now clear and finalized to me, not only through this vision of the floodgates, but also through visiting the Noah's ark replica. God was saying these were the days like Noah knew. And it was time to prepare an ark made of His Presence by worshipping Him and interceding fervently. This would be our protection and prevent many from being swept away by wickedness.

I tried to go back to sleep but it was quite a chore. I was thankful I did not have to drive the long hours back. When I returned from the Christmas trip God pressed my spirit to buy a hand drum. I put it off a few days but finally visited the music store. I walked away with a 12-inch djembe! I thought, "This is going to be interesting."

MY STRATEGIC GATE

It was now January 2013 and I was emblazoned with the fear of the Lord! The floodgates revelation rocked my world, but so did advice from a close friend, who at the time was key to my existence in New York. I was told I should not instruct but pray only, because I had nothing to teach. I had ability but needed to discover it fully. This one was concerned because God was opening many doors of influence and they didn't want me ruining the opportunities. This advice was a direct contradiction to my guidelines from the Lord. I was also criticized for my "ministry of offense" because the Lord had commissioned me to confront corruption and not to worry about offending people.

I wished I had listened to the Holy Spirit weeks prior when He told me to draw back from this friendship. Unfortunately, I didn't, and now I had no choice but to cease all communication. I was in a critical birthing phase and these expressed opinions were toxic to my assignment. My heart was crushed, as I loved this one dearly.

If I learned one thing, it is man always has an agenda for God's anointing. When faced with the decision to keep His blessing or a person's approval, the latter is always a dead end!

NEW YORK'S THIRD PRAYER SCHOOL

5 DAYS LATER: After the rendezvous pronouncing I had nothing to teach, I pressed on to hold a two-day school in a new city, followed by a twenty-four hour worship segment. As I entered this sanctuary on the first night, some deacons were present from the overseer church, as well as a few regional leaders from other cities.

I pulled the host pastor aside, "I have a very strong word to speak before I teach on prayer. You can stop me if it is too much and I will leave peacefully. But I must give the word."

He said, "Go for it."

The service began. Boldness came upon me and words flowed from my spirit.

"God is dealing with the fear of man this year in the churches of America and in our prayer rooms. We cannot consider how we appear to those around us; whether or not we offend someone is irrelevant. If we do something different than what man dictates can be done in a church service or a prayer meeting, so be it. We must have power! People don't know how to pray because they never pray. If Christians prayed, they would know what to do in prayer gatherings.

Our churches are overrun with insecure leaders more interested in guarding their position than having powerful intercession. Effective prayer is even halted if someone is more anointed than leadership. Also, many meetings are ended if something is done beyond their control. The enemy has sown tares in the church and we have bought into it. We've set our traditions around these tares and now our churches are so bound up that we are afraid to do anything outside of the box.

We must break out of the boxes of how our services look. The book of Acts was a demonstration of power because people sought the Lord. People in churches today no longer seek the Lord; they are busy holding services! They sit and watch others seek the Lord or listen to others tell them what to do. There is very little interaction with God; there is more consideration for taking offerings, displaying flawless songs and preaching.

God's idea of gathering His people was never intended to be thirty minutes of perfectly prepared songs sung by musicians more concerned with their appearance than pleasing God. It was never meant to exemplify entertaining sermons, while people sit like drones and leave like robots, bearing no fruit or power in their lives. Some one needs to blow the whistle and stop this! It's not working! We're losing a nation because of our traditions! We need God! All of us! Jesus didn't suffer and die upon a cross so we could have this sorry display of Christianity!"

This was the nature of things I spoke for forty-five minutes. Then I proceeded with the rest of my teaching on prayer. The host pastor's wife was upstairs listening. She figured she and her husband would now lose their jobs, (and place to live) because my conclusions were so strong against church structures.

After I finished speaking, on my way out, I walked through the congregation seats. A concerned pastor advised me to record the meetings so that no one could twist my words. She was afraid they would be used against me. I told her no, I stand with God. Let them speak whatever they want. Obviously, I had had a little transition since my last prayer school. In the previous city I was not so confrontational and this leader was a little shocked. But the host pastor encouraged me to let it stand; it was God. So we all left for the night.

The second night, the deacons were back and even more people came. I finished the prayer school and we launched straight into twenty-four hours of continual worship. As the music began, I called the congregants to the altar for intercession. It flooded with people. I commanded everyone to speak in tongues while I put my hand on their heads. I, too, was praying in the same manner. The place roared with power.

One woman was healed instantly as I touched her. She said fire shot from my hand and wrapped her head. The pain had been on one side for quite some time; it was now gone. She also had a three-month, persisting pain in her right shoulder blade. The doctors told her it was a nerve issue and there was nothing they could do, but Jesus healed her of that too!

Early the next morning I arrived back, and parked near the host church, only to be greeted by the woman who shouted, "I'm still healed! No pain!"

Upon my entry to the sanctuary, the Presence of God hovered strong; the musicians had played before the Lord all night. An older man was about to take the stage with his guitar. I asked to pray over him. (I had no idea he was a deacon of the overseer church!) I firmly exhorted him not to play rhetoric sheet music but flow spontaneously, loving the Lord. He seemed a bit put off.

But when he began, it was most traditional. I wondered if he heard a word I said, as thirty minutes slowly clicked by. About that time, the music stopped. There was silence. I looked up and saw the deacon's arms extended straight up in the air. His guitar hung on his waist. Rivers of tears were streaming down his face. He tried to speak through broken words, but the emotion of God had consumed him. He began to worship; I was enthralled!

This twenty-four hour idea came together at the last minute. Musicians had been called from the entire region in hopes they would play their instruments before the Lord. And come they did, many of them! Those who bore decades of offense even came.

The next morning was a Sunday. It was time for those who came to the prayer school/worship event attend the morning service of their overseer church. There was a mighty move of God. Many flooded the altar, speaking in tongues, as the Presence was so strong, people fell upon the floor. I was not there, but was told the church got rocked. The host pastor couldn't wait to attend the big church's weekly prayer to witness the transformation.

I spent that day and the next two, holed up in a hotel room, exhausted. I felt as if I had given physical birth. Reports continued to file in of the changed lives. People were being gripped with intercession. One individual, while preparing for work early in the morning, crumpled to the floor in sudden travail for the city. Many other stories of personal transformations compiled. This is another report I received from ground zero:

A few worship leaders were bringing some ELAM ministry school students who were having their week of prayer. They had been following all the stuff that was happening and were getting blazed up on Jesus, as their campus too, was getting rocked.

7 DAYS LATER: I was contacted by the host pastor with a short but pointed message, "Had a meeting last night. The government of the church is changing; passion has overtaken control! Thank you for staying the course. Be encouraged, that no matter the cost, it is worth it."

TWO WEEKS LATER: I received an email, recapping the changes that had occurred. "The region has been rescued/awakened and is currently being elevated to heavenly places, by way of intense passion for God, and prayer is fueling the process. Each time we are gathering for prayer there is a literal feeling, a sense of a close heaven; like tangibly. The testimony is vast, but in a nutshell, what we are seeing is people being healed, having visions and dreams.

Two people have reported, that as they are entering the region, they witnessed it being transformed. Things becoming brighter, colors, farms producing abundance, houses and buildings that are broken down, appear as brand new. Families are increasing and singing together, praises to the Lord. Basically we are just spending our days face down, laid out at the feet of the Father. All that we are saying or doing is what He is saying and doing, it's not about us; it's for us.

Since the 24-worship event, we have been opening the doors every evening, and all day on the weekends, with no agenda, but to listen and to be with Him. We aren't worried about numbers, or any of the normal church garbage, our only motivation is to live in His presence, and to see people taste of Him. And, know that He is good. I have heard nothing from the Lord about stopping or changing anything; I am just witnessing God do awesome stuff with His kids. I'm not sure where this is going but I know it's not going back to "doing church". I know that some seriously, good God-stuff has been released, and fostering this, will be done at His feet."

As it turned out, the very message everyone feared would cause trouble was the very thing that brought repentance and life. Two years later, I was told some of the people and different situations in the community can be traced back to that time.

A KEY LEADER

A FEW DAYS LATER: I was invited to attend a regional gathering in Niagara Falls. But the day of the meeting, the Buffalo prayer leader who invited me was struck with severe pain. I, too, did not feel well. Plus, I was not fond of driving in piles of snow at night! We decided not to go. Then her husband (uncharacteristically) called her from work.

"I think you should attend the meeting in Niagara Falls." He told her.

After that, we pressed through our physical symptoms and started for the Falls. A little while later, we parked and made our way through the dark, snowy street of a neighborhood. As I walked up the entrance, a beautiful African American woman with a sweet smile greeted me. I connected with her in the Spirit, instantly! I found out she was the leader of the packed-out meeting. Afterwards, we sat together and I told her what the Lord had said about America. She said she could see it in my eyes, and then invited me to speak at her gathering in a few weeks.

32

Within days, she phoned a leader in Geneva, "You need to have this girl speak."

Instantly, another regional meeting was set, this time in Geneva. It would be in four weeks. Next, she called a statewide leader,

"You need to have this lady hold a prayer school at your ministry school." So that event was scheduled too, for seven weeks out.

NEW YORK'S WELLS

In the meantime, I remained in western New York attending meetings and waiting for my next school in February. The snow was atrocious! One cold morning I drove to the nearest town for coffee and prayer in my car. I sat in a parking lot, thinking. I was off to a slow start and had no backdrop for what I was doing. I had held only three prayer schools in New York and struggled with the practicality of uncapping spiritual wells. I was also very puzzled at why God had not given a word for each individual city. But as I sat there pondering, I realized He had been speaking, I just needed eyes to see beyond the surface.

As I walked among the people, I noticed New Yorkers in upstate were a different breed altogether. They possessed an unusual tenacity and were extremely resilient, like they could walk through flames and not even flinch. This amazed me. I also spotted a revival "look" on their faces. And I mean, all of them! I saw it everywhere I went, in the supermarkets, at gas stations and in churches. It was odd because most of them were not even born-again. I could not figure out the mystery.

Then interrupting my thoughts, the Lord seemed to shout, "Tracey! It's in the land!"

Oh my goodness! How did I not see this before? It opened to me like a clear blue sky: the lion roaring, the Finney grave, the revival faces. My mind ran quickly; the phrase, the phrase! Since my arrival in New York, the words that greeted my immediate entrance to nearly every meeting: "Charles Finney was here."

I quickly did some research on my iphone and discovered Charles Finney was a New York preacher, and not only a preacher, but also the main guy responsible for America's second great awakening! I had no idea. Come to find out, the strangely named cities he visited were in New York, not England! The Lord flooded me with more revelation, melding each puzzle piece. The wells He sent me to uncap were multi-dimensional.

First, it was the leaders I was encountering. Each had a well of spiritual heritage dug through years of intimacy with God. But the dirt of disappointments, sickness, betrayals, and even death, had covered up these cisterns. (This was likened to the biblical wells Abraham dug, when later, during his son's life the Philistines filled them with dirt. But his firstborn, Isaac, uncapped them so the water could flow again.)

These people needed to flow again spiritually speaking, and release the promise of God for their lives and regions! It would happen only one way, by the Holy Spirit. Through intercession and apostolic authority these powerful leaders would be uncapped to release revival and awakening. God was rising up a new leadership in New York. I couldn't wait to see its fruition! Then, the next piece was revealed.

"Uncap the Finney well!" God exclaimed.

That's why I had to stop by the man's grave. My very path was the voiceless tone of God. He wanted another great awakening in America and knew this land and territory still retained the residue. It was time once again, to spread the fire!

The next part clicked in place. It was the lion roaring from the New York mountains. Just as a lion is the greatest voice in the jungle, so was New York to the land of America. This was the reason I had not received any more words for specific cities. The well was the entire state of New York! The NYSE was here and so was the most influential fashion industry. New Yorkers were tenacious, making them warriors by nature. And the Finney well was in New York!

God said, "Tracey, he left it in the land!" I was elated. If these components united and unleashed the Presence of God, it would be like a lion roaring over America. And no lion's roar can be ignored. The "voices" manipulating for control of our nation would be silenced if New York were uncapped! As I mused over my newfound revelation, a scheduled phone call came from my strategic friend, (the one who gave me the word about the reformer's anointing oil). While we talked, I looked through my windshield at the mounds of snow contrasting the sunny day.

As usual she wasted no time, "There's something in the land for you, Tracey. There is something in the land of New York that resonates with your spirit. There is a reciprocation taking place. You're picking up something from the land as well as leaving behind a deposit."

I knew it was the Finney well, but she did not. From here on I realized I could not leave New York until the Lord released me. He told me to stay until the impartation was complete, because one day I would carry it to the rest of the nation.

THE INTERVIEW

During these snowy weeks in western New York, it was time for my TV interview at the studio. I arrived mid-morning and was not too nervous until I realized who was facilitating my segment. It was a prominent minister. I took a deep breath and sat before him so we could prepare. He asked question after question about my life. I could tell he was rather experienced; he was so calm. After a few minutes they ushered us onto the stage inside the taping studio. We convened at a tall, round table with water-filled coffee cups. There we sat, a well-known minister and a hairdresser from Oklahoma. My first book lay on the table before us. I stared at the cover, which displayed my face painted with Native American war paint. I looked back up at him, silent. He mentioned he had heard of me, but was too busy to oblige his friends' requests that we meet. (But God saw to it.) Then the interview began.

The first phrases were personal in nature. Then, an out of place statement, "You are well-spoken. You could stand before thousands. You are a Joyce Meyer or a Marilyn Hickey." Why would I go to the unknown, small groups? As soon as possible I steered the conversation away from myself, towards America. I informed him the intercessors were the rudder for the nation. His reply was something about the general public expecting Billy Graham or others like him, to be the rudder. This was a different concept for me. I replied the intercessors and worshipers had the greatest voice because of their intimacy with God.

Then, when the minister brought up the one who labored with Finney in prayer, tears flooded my eyes. He quickly stretched the allotted time for the interview, and without prior permission, too. Suddenly, more space was given for me to finish my train of thought. The conversation progressed further. The glory grew thick. Now the producer was stretching the allotted time. After it was all said and done, I left the stage and the cameraperson trailed me; gripped to pray for America. Others to expressed the same! Then the minister approached me, asking for a lunch meeting…that never happened. Ha-ha!

TURNING TABLES

One of the meetings I attended while in western New York was a worship and prayer gathering. I was excited to join in, but as the day arrived, my spirit grew agitated. The Lord was bombarding me with provocative thoughts concerning the state of the church. He was specifically inciting the boldness of Elijah. This was not shocking, as He had already told me to confront lukewarmness. Obviously, it was still a fresh command!

When evening set in, I joined a pastor for the drive. We arrived on time and sat near the side. As the meeting progressed, and the longer I sat there, the more I noticed. The attendees appeared like drones. The words from the microphone sounded great, but demonstration was lacking. They were asking for revival over and over, but there was no fire. It was made known that the microphone was open, so I asked to pray. And with permission, I began to speak. I asked God to give the people an understanding of true revival. It was not mere words but a passion and a demonstration. Then I did the unfathomable; I spoke in other tongues!

I was hoping they would join me and experience a true, reviving Presence. But as I prayed, I felt huge resistance in the room. Perplexing indeed. The atmosphere clearly conveyed they wanted a certain arrangement, and I had brought something contrary. So I sat down.

Then someone whispered, "I think they cut your microphone."

I left the meeting early and shook the dust from my feet. But little did I know, that one act would cause such uproar. That night, I dreamed I was inside of a huge tower.

There were two Tyrannosaurus Rexes outside. One reptile began shaking the building with his roar and clawing at me. He reached right into the edifice, through the opening at the top. He was also trying to maul me with his teeth, when the other dinosaur appeared on the scene. They both tried to devour me, coming within inches of my skin. I was hunched down where the wall and floor met, screaming and crying. There was nowhere to hide, as the tower was empty.

I awoke unscathed, and glad it was only a dream! But soon I was receiving rebukes. The man who was the leader of the group indirectly came after me. He wanted an apology and to know about my "covering". He was meeting with other people and discussing me. My spirit immediately deferred to God. Then, a leader came to my aid, "Jesus didn't apologize when He over-turned the tables."
I was thankful for the recognition but also was concerned a bad reputation would precede me and stop the assignment. God told me to keep my mouth shut and move forward. So I stayed out of that city for the most part, as they loved praise from man more than glorifying God.

One morning, as I was battling fear from the persecution this minister was stirring up, the Lord spoke, "You have nothing to worry about, you are safe. It is for him that you should be concerned, because right up until the day the door shut on the ark, people were eating, drinking and marrying."

Right then my perception changed toward ministers who attacked me. I began to pray for the man, that he would awaken to the urgency of the hour before a flood came and swept him and his following away. He seemed so pompous, confident that he was right. It was apparent he didn't want me following the Lord unless he approved of the method.

One of the things I've learned about encounters like this is God is giving people a chance to experience awakening and revival. But it requires they put aside their scheduled agendas. Most refuse. Then they miss their moment of visitation, much like those in Israel when Jesus came to the earth. I'm sure I was labeled rebellious and doing my own thing. But God was blazing reformation in my spirit that night and would have spread it like a forest fire.

BRADFORD, PENNSYLVANIA

TWO WEEKS LATER: It was time for the prayer school in Bradford! This was a two-nighter. As I drove into the city that first night, I could hear evil spirits taunting me,

"Get out!" they said. "Get out of here."

Fear wrapped my body. I felt it in my bones. I parked my car in McDonald's parking lot and stood on the snow-packed ground. I could still hear the demonic chatter in the mountains surrounding me. I wished someone could have been with me for comfort; it was an awful feeling. But I pressed on. A few minutes later, I arrived at the church and was introduced to the pastors. They seemed sweet and loving. When I walked through the congregation toward the front, there were more in attendance than I expected. After the intro, I took the microphone and started singing without an instrument. I was trying to shift the atmosphere and silence the demonic ranting. It was a struggle, so I walked behind the drum cage and began a beat with my hand, while I continued to sing. Finally, light scattered!

I finished the first night and on my way out, a woman who said I was needed in Bath, New York greeted me. I gave her my information and within a week a date was set for a prayer school in Bath. (It would be held the same weekend as the ministry school. Two schools, in two cities, in three days!)

When I finished the second night in Bradford, I had a first-time experience. After calling everyone to the altar I anointed them with oil and played a song from my computer. The microphone was resting on its tiny speaker so it could be heard over the big system. It wasn't professional, but God led it. Obviously, someone didn't like the ma and pa display because the microphone was switched off, and then replaced with radio-style music. The Holy Spirit left the building!

God said to me, "You can leave now."

I was afraid, "Lord, what did I do wrong?"

He said, "They didn't honor you and I won't honor them."

I couldn't leave fast enough but my host was addressing the congregation. I waited a few more minutes and informed her to close out the service. I walked away that night feeling peculiar. But I pressed on. The next day, I was pondering the events and the Lord said,

"Go back to that city and do seven nights of prayer."

So I called my host friend, who inquired of the Lord. She suggested we schedule each night at a different location. "Great!" I said. So the time was set, it would be in a few weeks.

NIAGARA FALLS

12 HOURS LATER: I traveled to Ohio for a week or so, and then drove back to New York on a Thursday. I was scheduled to speak that night in Niagara Falls. It was the same location I had attended in January, except this time, I was the speaker. I talked on the baptism of fire! Specifically, speaking in tongues with results likened to lighting. I shared the biblical instance of John the Baptist when he spoke of Jesus, the coming Messiah. I read Matthew 3:11 to everyone and focused on the last phrase which tells us Jesus will baptize us with Holy Spirit and fire.

When I googled the definition in the original translation, I discovered three descriptions for the word fire. One of them was lightning. The word lightning grabbed my attention because it was stated as being figurative or literal. This was my homily for the night:

Jesus left the earth and gave us the authority to access all of heaven and to be filled with His ability and presence like a fire. I believe He intended nothing to remain in our vessels but His kingdom power and glory, which manifests when we pray in tongues. Praying in other tongues is a weapon! And we must learn to wield it and utilize it to its fullest ability. Then, when this weapon is operating at its greatest potential, our spirit words will be as lightning; quick, powerful and effective! They will be sharp and piercing, dividing truth from injustice.

In order to have quick and powerful tongues we must have a powerful spirit. And our spirit becomes powerful through praying in tongues, extensively. If our spirit is not powerful we will not have explosive results. If our spirit *is* powerful, the battle will be short and effortless. Then, we will decree a thing and it will be established. Then, we will release His Presence from our spirit and it will accomplish that which it was sent forth to do. We must carry it to release it! If we don't carry power, no power will be released. So we see here that if the fire inside is like lightning, it should come out like lightning!

ANOINTING WITH OIL

After I delivered the above revelation, I called everyone who wanted prayer to stand before me at the podium, one at a time. I would anoint with oil and God would send His fire. Many wanted prayer, so this lasted for a bit. When we finished, a quite aged pastor said to me, "That is the most powerful message I have ever heard. I will never be the same again. I am going back to my congregation and tell them. I am going to tell everyone!"

I was so blessed and thankful for fruit that would remain. As soon as he finished, a woman in her eighties stood. She desired the attention of the whole room. Then, through a religious spirit, she undermined my teaching on the baptism of fire. "It's all in the *spoken word*," she said over and over, emphasizing the quoting of scriptures to see the kingdom.

The message I delivered was one of utter transformation according to the possession of God's Spirit. The argument she was enforcing skipped this intimacy with God in order to salve the conscience through scripture repetition. Ah! I was frustrated. The whole room erupted in a verbal discourse. I tried to defend the truth but felt I was beating the air. The leader who invited me to the group mildly set her straight, enforcing that no where in my message was I saying we didn't need scriptures.

Before I left, a leader sitting nearby invited me to come to his city the next night and teach at his intercession group. I accepted and took his church's address. Then, I headed out into the snow for another late-night, hour drive back to my host home. I fell asleep satisfied but bewildered at the dishonor of the eighty-year-old woman.

WILLIAMSVILLE

24 HOURS LATER: I was to speak in Williamsville, New York. It was a nice, sunny day so the drive was pleasant. I arrived at night to see a large, beautiful church. Across the street was a small building where I entered and found a room full of hungry

intercessors! Rather than beginning our time with teaching, I stood up and just started praying in tongues. I prayed with fire and no English for quite a lengthy time. I think the abruptness was a bit uncomfortable for them, but they were desperate for more of God and followed suit. My thought process: I would only be with them a short while, so I was imparting a large measure all at once. I walked around the room, laying hands on them as I prayed. This was another night of fire! The evening ended all too soon, then I was on my way. I arrived at my sleeping quarters very, late again. I had a few days to rest before returning to Pennsylvania for a week of prayer.

7 DAYS ABLAZE FOR BRADFORD

52 HOURS LATER: The regional leader contacted me a couple of days before the week of prayer in Bradford. While she was scheduling churches for a prayer explosion, a viper raised its head, "Sorry, we have to cancel the meeting for intercession."

After this pastor spoke out, so did a few others. The churches were shutting me out! We soon discovered someone had attended the prayer school and was talking about me. Something I said was being twisted. So the regional leader and I decided to take it to the homes. And it was ever so powerful. Seven nights straight we gathered! Each night we prayed in tongues for nearly two hours. We were filled with fire and more fire. Each gathering seemed to build upon the next. The first evening was at a pregnancy center, and the next, a home in downtown, then another house outside of town. At the end of the week a church opened up just across the New York border.

During this week, I had an unusual occurrence. I skipped one of our nights of prayer for a meeting in another city, so I was resting in the afternoon before the trip. All of a sudden, I heard a man's name in my spirit. Quickly, I typed it out and saved in my phone. I asked if anyone knew him but no one did. Then I searched the Internet, I came up with nothing. So, I shelved it and drove to the other city. Afterwards, I returned to finish the week of prayer in Bradford.

Toward the end of the week we met in a home just outside of town. The attendance in this meeting increased, making it difficult for everyone to be on the same page while we prayed. So I grabbed a rhythm with heal of my boot on the wooden floors, and pounded out a cadence. I clapped and sang war-like songs in other tongues. The atmosphere shifted and pulled everyone into powerful intercession! In the midst of this intense environment, I noticed some older, teen-age girls walking back and forth through the corner of the room. It was quite a distraction. They were not praying with us, just staring. This went on for several minutes until their mom asked if I would pray with them.

"Only by their permission," I said.

As the oldest girl stood before me, I inquired of her salvation. She assured me she was born-again. I asked if she was filled with the Holy Spirit. Her reply baffled me. From her bedroom, she heard my boots on the wooden floor and my singing in tongues. It grabbed her attention, so she began to stomp her feet like me and sing. That's when she started to speak in tongues, for the first time!

She was baptized in the Holy Spirit without anyone praying for her. Next, her sister stood before me. I asked of her salvation. She too, assured me she was born-again. Then we prayed for her to receive the baptism of the Holy Spirit. Instantly, she spoke in tongues. This concluded our night at the little house outside of town. I realized the biggest distractions are sometimes the greatest blessings!

ONE YEAR LATER

One year later I received a phone call from the regional leader in this city. She was elated. She had dreamed big for her town to experience revival, but what was happening was far beyond her vision. It all began a year prior when we walked the main strip. I had forgotten about it until she reminded me!

"Let's walk main street and anoint every door with oil, commanding Christian businesses to open up down here." I said to her. She was on it! So we trekked through the snow up and down the sidewalks. We went inside of every crevice of the every storefront, and the reformer's anointing oil was placed every so carefully. Afterwards, we went about our business as usual. Soon my week was over in Bradford and I moved on to the next city.

So here's the rundown of what happened in less than a year. God spoke to the regional leader to open a small business on main street. (She was the first fulfillment of our oil venture!) She was witnessing to the community from her place at the gates. Next, another Christian business opened up. Then, the industry bringing in all the riff-raff at the end of the street, moved *out*. (It was drawing people who vandalized the properties. And during the city meetings, the business owners kept complaining it was not good for their commerce. So this was huge!) The city then beautified the property and installed cameras to prevent anymore the damage.

The next thing that happened could only be God. A movie company decided to use Bradford as the backdrop for a film! So they came into town and renovated the street just behind the retail stores, and parallel to main street. (It was on the backside of all the businesses we prayed over.) The renovations included the road, the sidewalks and even the street lamps being replaced with stunning ornamentation. Even the storefronts on that side were refurbished.

Now, as if that isn't enough, the regional leader started proclaiming, "In one year's time, you are not going recognize this place!" And of course the fulfillment of her prophecy came true. The movie company announced they decided to redo all of main street too! (And it would take exactly *a year*.) This was great, but there's more. The owner of the movie theatre next to her shop decided to run some Christian films. The place packed out, so repeat showings were induced. Then, a young girl came into to my friend's shop, "I feel like I'm supposed to go into the movie and preach!" My friend said, go.

In the middle of all of this, a city administrator happened by my friend's shop too. This person didn't know "what was going on around there." But, while the two were chatting, it was revealed the administrator was returning to church after years of absence. During the conversation about the happenings, it was made known finances were available to open a coffee shop on main street; someone just needed to run it. Well, recently the regional leader discovered a Christian girl who wanted to manage a coffee spot. She just needed the finances. (Now if the coffee shop idea went beyond opportunity, it would mean another Christian business opened on main street!)

My friend was talking fast; the next topic of renovation flew boldly out of her mouth, "The old regime pastors are being moved out of the churches! And new young pastors, who are on fire and the real deal are replacing them."

Wow. Every sect of society was being rocked. The business community, the churches and even the economy was boosted. While these stories were rolling I began to cry. I sat in bed one year later, still recovering from exhaustion. I thought if I hadn't obeyed God, none of this would have ever happened. I was glad I did not listen to the intercessor in Arkansas who told me to go back home! After this, I was talking to a pastor in western New York. I asked if she heard what happened in Bradford. She hadn't.

But after I told her, she said, "Tracey, this is Isaiah 58; restorer of the streets to dwell in."

Profound. This is what reclaiming cities and nations looks like. Every crevice of society will be transformed when God's people, walking in humility, purity, and authority decide to rescue the souls of a land. Those who pay the price will have greatest voice.

4

CENTRAL NEW YORK

GENEVA, NOT SWITZERLAND

9 HOURS LATER: I drove quite a distance from my current stomping grounds of western New York. Even though I slept, I was so, so tired. I arrived in downtown Geneva, parked on the street and hiked up the hill, sporting my heavy drum, my Mac and my bible. It took a few minutes to find the place but I finally discovered the triple-story home nestled between a row of others.

The beautiful Boston-style house was stunning. I climbed the steps to the front door and rang the bell. An odd looking, gray-headed woman answered. I asked if the leader of the meeting was available. The lady responded rather vague and disrespectful.

Her actions clearly conveyed, "Who are you to talk to the leader? You're just a kid."

She was not obliging at all and walked off. So I wandered around the multi-level home asking for the leader of the meeting. When I found her I introduced myself. She didn't say much, and the event began shortly thereafter. Quite a few people packed the top floor. I was excited to meet these souls because I had an encounter a few days prior.

It was 4 a.m. and I was awakened by the sound of blasting elephant trunks. To me it was audible. The Lord quickly said,

"The people you are about to meet will be your elephants."

A little perplexed, I wondered what it meant. Then He reminded me of a theatrical depiction of Noah's ark. In the film, Noah reached a place where he was not strong enough to lift the beams to finish the task. That's when the elephants came to help. They were sturdy and could lift heavy things. What an amazing parallel!

I was excited to tell them, but the meeting was in full swing and had been going for a few hours. Since the leader didn't convey much to me, I decided to relinquish the probability of speaking and enjoy the atmosphere. Then about thirty minutes before the end, she stopped the music and asked if I had anything to share. Before I expounded on the elephant word, I spoke about intercession coming from the heart. If it didn't come from the heart it wasn't true intercession! Those who simply make decrees or recite list prayers, minus a passion for God are pointless displays of prayer. (I had a word of knowledge that those in the room were from a company of prophetic people who operated this way. But I did not tell them.)

I spoke intensely, sharing further we could not continue bowing to the fear of man in our churches. I made clear this was America's problem. Then I shared the dream about the three bronze-colored floodgates. The revelation gripped them. Word got back to me that some were awakened at 3:33 a.m. after hearing this warning. (And on a side note, many people that opened their homes to me relayed their difficulty in sleeping too. Awakening accompanied my travels in more than one-way!) Finally, I revealed the elephant parable, which increased their confidence greatly.

Now, even though I had brought my drum, I did not have the courage to play it. So I anointed with oil all who were present, except the odd-looking woman who greeted me at the door. She was offended by my humility and excused herself from the blessing. When I finished praying over the people, intercession became electric in the atmosphere! After this weekend, my new home base moved from the Buffalo region to Geneva. From here, I traveled to dozens of cities across central and northern New York during the months of March, April and May 2013.

THE BORDER TOWN

24 HOURS LATER: I drove from Geneva back to Bradford to finish off the week of prayer. The last night would be held in a small church located on the Pennsylvania-New York border. This was strategic because of the many prophecies about revival fire along the boundary. I suspected God was having us uncap that well too! During this meeting the people were so involved in intercession that one could not tell if there was a facilitator. I know this because the pastor showed up late and commented about the powerful gathering that no one was leading!

THE RETREAT

Afterwards, I drove another late night, (over two hours) back to Geneva. I slept there, and then the next day I retreated to Toledo for a worship gathering. While I was in Ohio, a spontaneous prayer meeting was called on my behalf. A handful of prophets and leaders took it upon themselves to douse me in the fires of intercession. And boy was I thankful! The most unforgettable prophetic word was released over my life that night. And I would be amiss if I left out its relevance in this manuscript. It was quite significant to my one-year mission, and for me personally; it helped to unravel the mysteries that were unfolding. So when the host prophet of the meeting began to speak, he boldly proclaimed the following, power-packed revelation. (I sat quietly in the middle of the room, listening.)

FORESIGHT

"You will be able to see close up, because you will have already seen from far away. God is going to give you the read of a place before you arrive, so you can leave one place and go immediately to another place, and you will already have prepared ahead of time in the Spirit. Because from miles away, from the comfort of your living room you will see these places, and you will be able to articulately say what it is God is saying. You will be able to put it to pencil and paper. You'll be able to see it in the Spirit. And you will have already dealt with it in your heart. You will have already prepared to deal with what it is that you will see in these places. And it's important, because you're not just going to go to metropolises; you're going to small towns. You're going to places that are wide spots in the road..."

THE MAPPING

"...And God is going to give you impromptu meetings; you're going to sit at roadside diners or taverns. And you're going to sit down in places; and the Presence and the conviction of the Father will be so strong over you, that people in these places will respond to Jesus without your words. And you will lead them and you will pray over them. And you will seal them to the Father. You will seal them on your spaces. Because God is not just giving you the cities, He's giving you the roads. He's giving you the highways. He's giving you the interstates. He's giving you the travel plans. And He's carefully, carefully mapping out your feet. Do not worry whether the places you have invitations have been planned by the Father. For the Father is guiding the hands of the inviters. He's guiding the invitations from His end, from His perspective; from heaven."

ROTATIONS

Then, for several minutes this prophet began to walk around the perimeter of the room. After his silence he announced,

"Every time I made the full rotation, the Holy Spirit shouted out to me, (in my spirit) the number of the time. And as soon as I would walk around the room and hit the full rotation, I'd hear one, two, three. But by the time I got to the later rotations, by the time I hit one rotation I would hear the next number, immediately. It was accelerating as I was walking around the room. And I searched through the scriptures for 'seven times'..."

SEVEN TIMES

"...I found dozens of passages: He Himself went before them bowing down to the ground, *seven times*...The priest shall dip his finger in the blood and sprinkle it *seven times*... *Seven times*, it will be cleansed by him from the leprous disease... Dip the right finger that is on the oil of his left, sprinkle oil *seven times* before the Lord... He shall provide with the right finger *seven times* oil on the cedar wood, and hyssop and scarlet yarn, *seven times*... All through the book of Leviticus: Eleazar the priest took blood on his fingers and sprinkled it *seven times*. And then it says in Joshua that the priests shall bear *seven* rams horns before the ark, and on the *seventh* day, you shall march around the city, *seven times*. And on the *seventh* day they rose early, and at the dawn they marched around the city in the same manner, *seven times*. And it was on that day they marched around the city, *seven times*..."

MARCHING

"...I just get the idea that there is something that has been marched around you, and the Father is marching, and He is marching and He is marching. And He is declaring the numbers of the rotations in seasons. *Seven times*, He has declared over you numbers before the Lord, the numbers that have come forth tonight over you. He is declaring over you that you have marched *seven times* before the Lord. You have dipped your hair before His altar in the Presence of His mighty Self. *Seven times*, you have laid yourself; you have prostrated before the Lord. And the Lord declares over you that just as Joshua and his priests marched around the city *seven times*, *seven days*, God is saying over you that the walls are beginning to *rattle* and *shake*. You need to be ready for it is accelerating before the Lord.

The Lord is saying that even as you have come around the city, you have heard the number of the second rotation immediately in your spirit. You have heard God accelerating the cry; and *seven times* you've come before Him. And *seven times* you have prostrated yourself before Him. And *seven times* the Father has dipped His fingers in the blood of His Son, and the oil of His Presence, and the wine of His healing, and the water of His redemption. And He has placed it over you, *seven times...*"

THE FATHER'S WORDS

"...The Father says tonight that it is done. It is done in the heavens; it is done. And you will begin to see it in the earth. It has already begun to be declared to you by your friends, by your loved ones, by your prayer warriors. And Father says, in the Spirit, *seven times* you have come before Him. *Seven times* you laid before Him. *Seven times* you've been anointed by oil, and blood, and water in His Presence; *seven times.* Father also says you have cried before Him. *Seven tears* have been shed before Him, as you have cried out for the work of this planet, and for the work of yourself, and also for the work of those that you are coming before. And for the work that will be done by those that have ministered before you, as you have ministered before the Lord..."

CONSECUTIVE ANOINTINGS, CALLINGS AND GIFTINGS.

"The Father is giving you three more anointings. You will cry before Him for three more things. And as the first four came at the rotation; one, two, three, four; five, six and seven will happen at the beginning of the last rotation. It will be set in place. It will be accelerated. And the things that you have not seen yet, will come to you quickly. For Father has *seven callings* over you and three more callings/three more gifts have not been placed in your hands yet. But they have already been declared in His presence, they have already been written in a scroll. And those that run with the scrolls have already taken hold of the scrolls and they're beginning to run. The last three gifts that Father has placed in you are now going to be revealed at an accelerated basis. He's already declared it in the heavens. He's already had it written in His scroll. And He's already handed it to the courier to run..."

THE COURIER

"...And Father is saying over you that this courier is not being held back, for he is on a race. But is it not a race like a sprint; it is a marathon. And this courier is beginning to run up alongside of you. And you feel it in the Presence of the Lord right now; that if you reach out your hand, he'll hand you the first of the next three gifts; the baton in the Spirit. And I just get the idea that as you finish each rotation, the courier will come up behind you and put another gift in your hand. But you have to know, it's already been declared at the beginning of the previous lap; it's already there. So as soon as you hit lap four; gifts five, six, and seven are ready for you. And every time you make a lap, every time you make a lap in this race, God will hand you another tool, another gift, and He will reveal another of your callings..."

THE PLACING OF THE SEVENS

"...And the Father is just placing this over you: *seven callings*. You have prostrated yourself before the Lord *seven times*. You've laid yourself down, *seven times*. You've cried *seven tears*. And Father is saying over you do not grow weary in the last laps, because they will be faster and more accelerated than the first laps. And if you think you're tired now, you *will be tired*. For Father is putting in you legs like the legs of horses. He asked Jeremiah, if you can't run with people, how could you run with the horses? For the Father is giving you a new strength and a new wind. You will have to run with horses. But if you rely on your own strength you will not be able to race with men..."

A HAMMERED A TRUTH

"...For Father is saying over you that there is an anointing in the spirit. And like Elijah, who hitched up his garments, and who ran ahead of the clouds of rain, God is asking you today, will you hitch up your garments, will you run ahead? Because *seven years* have gone! And you have cried before the Lord! And you have asked Him for this season! Will you now quit your race! Or will you see in the Spirit with eyes that have been placed in your head from the Father's Presence? And will you see the cloud on the horizons?

And you will you hitch up your garments, and will you run ahead of the storm? For Father is sending rain. And it is rain that will revitalize parched lands. For as you walk through the fields and the country sides; entire generations, who have dealt in drought all of their lives [in the spirit], you will walk through, and you will run ahead of the rain that will revitalize their lives, their callings, and their ministries…"

WILL YOU HITCH UP YOUR GARMENTS?

"…But will you continue to run? Will you hitch up your garments, so that when you run through the neighborhoods, the small towns, and the big towns, in the cities, in the city centers of the metropolises, will you be willing to continue to run ahead of the storm? For Father says that if you will run He will provide the rain. And He will begin to pour out His rain upon lands that are parched. And you will declare the storm of the Lord of His Presence that is coming up alongside of you. And every time you make a full rotation He will give you another tool, another gift, another calling, for which you will be known for, far and wide.

Right now you have been known for prayer. You've been known in the past for healing. You have been known to say the Father's words boldly and with the authority of Jesus. You have walked in apostolic authority. You have those four gifts. But you have not received the last three gifts the Father has for you. And as you run these races the courier is already running up behind you. Can you hear his footsteps? He is ready to pass the scroll from the Father's Presence, from the Father's words, from the Father's finger to you. But you must hitch up your garments and run ahead of the storm.

You must be willing to run in circles, so that every time you run a lap, the courier will run up behind you and give you a scroll, another calling for which you will be known for. Authority, prayer, healing; God has given you those three gifts. Presence. God has given you the fourth gift, Presence. Your heart is ready. You've received the humility of the Father. And now it's time to run in regal royalty, garbed like an Olympic athlete, taking the scroll for the restoration, for the healing of the nations."

THE MYSTERIES MAKE SENSE

The layers of this revelation were so multi-dimensional and eternal, a finite mind could not possibly grasp the fullness of their intentions. But as I pondered the lengthy disclosure, a few things seemed to stand out.

The prophetic gifting would help me prepare for each city before I arrived. A clarion call for me to run ahead of the storm coming to America was evident. Also, I needed to decree the storm of the Lord He had promised to send over the land and the people. As I contemplated the mystery of the sevens, I realized the rotations were the "7 Days Ablaze". And the priest dipping his finger in the oil and blood for cleansing was Jesus, our High Priest, dipping His finger and placing it on the people as I anointed them with oil.

The part where, "I cried seven tears" made complete sense. And so did the phrase, "Seven years had gone and I had cried before the Lord and asked Him for this season!" These all spoke of the nuptial agreement I mentioned in chapter one. The miry pit lasted seven, long years. I cried myself to sleep nearly every night due to oppression and the dying of my destiny. I was called to birth revivals and awaken nations, but as long as I was stuck in that situation, I was going nowhere! Eventually the Lord rescued me, and though it was long ago, He was letting me know my destiny was being fully redeemed. He was putting me back where I belonged. After that night, I remained in Ohio for several days. Then I returned to Geneva to prepare for a meeting in another city.

RUSHVILLE

10 DAYS AFTER BRADFORD: Yesterday I was in Ohio, today I was in central New York in the back of an art studio/hair salon. I was invited to join a group of prophetic people who met every week for prayer. The fire fell intensely as I prophesied over the owner. It seemed the words would never end! Prophesying was not my custom, even though I could perceive many hearts. Evidently, what I said was extremely accurate and the woman was greatly encouraged.

CLIFTON SPRINGS

48 HOURS LATER: This was a one-time meeting, and a most glorious experience. Most of the people in this community could not make it to the prayer school scheduled for their area, so I went to the home group. The fire of God was very present. When I was finished, I ended up flat on my back roaring in laughter, barely able to walk to my SUV.

The history of this home and land its location was remarkable. One hundred years ago, the original owner started a hospital from the springs of water discovered in the area. People came from all over the world to soak in the waters, and more significantly, they came to the house I was teaching that night. Many famous revivalists walked the same wooden floors. They frequented the home and soaked in the tub upstairs. What a well!

CANANDAIGUA

FOUR DAYS LATER: I was invited to a meeting for intercessors in Canandaigua. Sorry, I don't remember much of it!

BATH

TWO DAYS LATER: I was scheduled to do a prayer school in Bath, New York. I arrived in the city during the evening and ninety minutes before the meeting. It was just enough time to have dinner with the regional leader. As I climbed the entrance stairs I was met by a shocked look, followed by the question that explained it,

"How old are you?"

This was embarrassing, as everyone seemed overly concerned with my age. I told her I was barely hanging onto my thirties. She took it to mean I had just turned thirty. This regional leader was quite a soul! She was old enough to be my mother and had more energy than most people half my age. Her story was rather riveting. She had been married to a Muslim for a few decades. Shortly after their nuptial agreement she became a Christian and had survived heavy

56

oppression, amongst other tough circumstances. After her husband passed from cancer, she flew out of the gate like a racehorse! She was excited to be able to organize gatherings and tell people about Jesus. (I noticed she had no anger and much love toward Muslims, but she did not possess an idolatrous tendency toward Islam. This amazed me.) God gave her so much favor across central New York it was astounding. Her gift was mobilizing pastors and leaders. And when she called a meeting, they all came!

After dinner, I drove to the Baptist church and found the fellowship hall packed out. I taught for two hours and concluded around 9 p.m. The next morning was Friday, and I rose very early to make sure I was cognitive for the all-day teaching, which began at 9:30 a.m. As was my custom, I sat in my SUV sipping coffee and praying. Suddenly, I noticed a fever in my body. My throat hurt severely and I was nauseated. I opened my mouth and saw white spots. Ugh! Strep throat. It was an hour before the morning session started, so I quickly texted the strongest prayer warriors I knew. They were in Oklahoma and Arkansas. Within thirty minutes my fever dropped and the white spots were smaller. Praise God! I didn't feel one hundred percent yet, but I decided to walk it off. I knew healing had set in.

I taught the early session, and then the rest of the day. I finished at 4 p.m. After I anointed everyone with oil, I set the dates for the seven nights of prayer for that city, making sure they scheduled seven different locations. Then, I set off for another city to start a new prayer school that night. It was an hour and a half drive and I was so hungry. So I raided a grocery store on my way out of town. I sat in the parking lot consuming hot peppers. I decided to try the spicy buggers instead of coffee! It was a brilliant idea. Once my taste buds were good and numb, I meandered through the rest of snowy, narrow roads to make it by 7 p.m. for the next meeting.

Here's one person's account concluding the school in Bath. I ran across it on the Internet, "God has commissioned Tracey to travel the country, teaching intercessors to pray effectively and fervently for revival. She has been drawn by God to study Charles Finney's revival work in NY, until she unlocks what God desires her to accomplish here! Knowing that Finney was up here, I'm sure she will eventually end up here! Please be praying for her to come to your area, too. Revivals are following what she is doing. Her mission is to train us, and move on. We've got the work to do, to unstop the wells of water under our individual cities. One of her visions was of wells under the cities that need to be released! Here's her email, if you'd like to get in contact with her, and I do hope you will."

THE MINISTRY SCHOOL IN CANANDAIGUA

3 HOURS LATER: I arrived exhausted but ready to teach. There were quite a few in attendance, and the sessions were being recorded by audio and video, which made me nervous. I finished that Friday evening session and drove thirty minutes back to a host home. The next morning was Saturday and it came early, as the class began at 9 a.m. There were even more in attendance than the night before. I felt humbled, as quite a few sat in another room where they could only hear me.

At the mid-morning break, the young man leading worship approached me. There was a coffee shop around the corner, would I like one? His words and twenty-something face were music to my ears! I so missed my younger friends. He was the first person I had seen in my meetings that was twenty-something. (Later, I realized this significance.) After lunch I taught a few more hours, and then concluded the school by anointing everyone with oil. I prayed in tongues fervently over each one, commanding them to do the same. This was a very powerful time!

While the people were leaving, I was approached by a man in the audience who was from a major university in New York. It was liberal, all the way to its roots. He told me the man who established it vowed to never have a Christian witness on the campus. He said that happened for the first time last year. Then he asked if I would come and teach. I was elated! After we concluded that conversation, I left for some take-out food and then headed to my abode for the night.

It was difficult to unwind and rest after so many hours, cities and days in intense warfare and intercession. The large amounts of coffee I drank to keep me alert were not so forgiving, either. I slept that Saturday night at a beautiful Inn in the country, but rose early the next morning; I just couldn't sleep. It was Sunday and I had the entire day off and also the next seven nights. I was looking forward to it so I could rest and recover from the past few days of intensity. But I hoped too soon! In the afternoon, the regional leader from Geneva brought to mind we had not set a week of prayer following the school in Canandaigua. She expressed a fervent desire to do it. Her city, Geneva was a short drive, so she could host the meetings. My flesh wanted to rest, but we started right away.

7 DAYS ABLAZE IN GENEVA

MONDAY, 18 HOURS LATER: 7 days a blaze began in Geneva. A few days into this week a man brought two teen-age boys with him. It was clear they knew nothing about prayer and probably didn't want to be there. Quite honestly they were a distraction for me! This was an intimate time for intercessors to pray effectively, it was not intended for outreach. But I obliged them. Then I explained what we were doing and why we were doing it. The response was bored stares perusing the place. So, I walked into a side room and knelt before the Lord, pouring my heart out to Him. That night ended with not such a huge breakthrough, or so I thought!

The next day, the report came that one of the teenagers from the night before had not been born-again. But during the meeting he walked over into the little side-room and saw Jesus standing there. Wow. I gave myself a silent rebuke for my tunnel vision and bad attitude.

5

APRIL BEGINS

ROCHESTER

I left Geneva late Monday morning for a meeting at noon. It was by invitation only and complied of four leaders from different ministries. I was excited to be in Rochester, as New Yorkers continually rehearsed this bustling city was affected most by Finney. It is said, ninety percent were Christians, and at the time the population was close to ten thousand. A minister told me the reason for Finney's success was his refusal to allow Masonry gatherings while he was present. This order came from the civil officials of the city with whom he met before doing any meetings. What influence.

Another interesting story was passed on to me from a leader who moved to a small town in central New York. During her first week in the city, she entered a Laundromat and a woman whom she did not know approached her. She offered to tell her why the town was so peaceful. The fact was Charles Finney had lived there for a few months. The community respected him so much they refused to build a bar. To that day, one hundred and fifty years later, there was no bar in the town. The leader relayed to me that after she moved away she heard the first one finally opened. It was at the end of a bowling alley, but it soon closed down. She said it was the love Finney had for the people that caused such respect.

Stories like these were on my mind as I entered the metropolis of Rochester. I didn't sense anything unusual in the atmosphere, that is until I walked into the meeting. When my feet hit the wooden floors of the large domed room, I felt the heritage in the earth. It was like I stepped into a time machine and went back nearly two centuries. I approached the couch and tears were falling from my face. Heat rushed over my head. I remained calm and smiled at everyone but I was in another realm. I prevented myself from wailing in prayer as I sat down. My mind flashed back to that first morning in New York at the pastor's kitchen table. This was the same feeling; it was something not of myself, but a sphere I walked into. God wanted me to feel it, sense it and tap it. It was a deep, deep well in the ground.

While the others were sharing, an hour passed by and I was still weeping. I barely heard the conversations because God was showing me their hearts. He was telling me to speak over their destinies; call them out, lay hands on them and put fire into their spirits. So, when I was asked to share at the end, I obeyed. In the process, the deep travail emerged. My core was pulsating the depths of God's heart. I couldn't kneel fast enough! When the palms of my hands landed on the floor's surface, they grew very hot.

While I was on my face, I loosed travailing tongues to the earth beneath and over the people of the city. They needed to fulfill their destinies and hear the cry of God to their generation! They must see His holiness and know His fire. I wailed and wailed until I thought I would embarrass myself. I wondered if those in the room knew the promise that lay beneath their feet. I wondered if they knew of God's desire to visit them again and birth a hunger that could not be quenched.

Finally, I pulled myself together and stood up to a holy fear in the room. Quietly I sat back down, yearning to return to the floor and stay until the room was riveted with fiery power. I have never felt such a tangible anointing from the ground as that day. Even now as I write this section, tears are my companions. There are no words to describe what I experienced in the cities of the burned-out district. God sensitized my spirit so much, I literally felt I was back in the 1800's. I picked up such an impartation, that by the end of my journey, I felt like I was wearing Finney's boots. At one point, I could here the sound of my treading feet in the unseen realm. It was like a "thud of revival" slapping the ground every time my soles touched the earth.

The Presence of God is real, and there is no space in time with Him Who has no beginning nor ending. I could hear the cries of intercession from saints gone by, and feel the fire that Finney carried and left behind. Prayers remain until they are fulfilled. What they did not see in their time, may we see in ours!

CORNELL UNIVERSITY

48 HOURS LATER: I was scheduled to have dinner in Ithaca with a couple that lived near the campus of Cornell University. The husband was the man who told me of its liberal beginnings. Some young people from Pennsylvania were also invited to the dinner. When I arrived, it didn't take long to realize we had the same ministry friends, as one of the guys blurted out from across the table,

"I thought you looked familiar!"

We had been a part of the same worship gathering in Washington D.C. a few years prior. What a fun evening in Ithaca. They had come to worship the Lord on campus all week. I felt like a spiritual mom and asked if I could pray over them. They excitedly said yes! So I imparted authority and more fire into their spirits. I wanted them to receive all I had and more! Afterwards, we adjoined on the campus for the worship event. Many students came and I enjoyed meeting new faces. As usual, I drove back to my temporary abode, long and late at night.

IRONDEQUOIT

12 HOURS LATER: I drove one hour to Irondequoit, a city just outside of Rochester. The first meeting was set for noon and would last until 4 p.m. I would be introduced to the city commissioner that afternoon! So I parked my SUV, and loaded into the car with the man who invited me and his wife. We drove to the back of the government building and quickly climbed the stairs to the Commissioner's office.

Inside, we prayed, and I shared with her the heart of my mission for America. She was a very sincere woman. Then the four of us united for a car drive around the city. We visited many strategic spots. Along the way, I saw a sign in the distance and asked about the plot of land. The car quickly came to a halt. We walked through the grass to read the title, "Gateway to the Continent". How intriguing. God had said He would send me to gate cities and gateway cities. This was the gateway to the entire continent! After this we returned, so the city commissioner could finish her work. House church started in two hours, and beforehand, I would have dinner with the leaders.

In the mean time, I started to run a fever. Ugh! It was strep throat trying to rear its ugly head again. I pressed through, as the Lord sustained me. After dinner, there was thirty minutes spare time, so I rested for about twenty of those, and then drove across the street for a coffee. I hoped the jolt would help me speak clearly, since my body was groggy from battling the fever.

That night at the house church, I shared on dreams of the heart. I encouraged the people to act on them, emphasizing it was not too late to accomplish their dreams. God would induce the supernatural, if only action would occur! Some of them received the breakthrough but others struggled to understand. No matter how hard I tried, I could not make the shift for them. They had to open their minds to what God was saying.

I left with cookies and snacks in hand for another late drive back. The dark country roads were soothing, but as usual, my nerves were on edge. My old SUV had a tail light out due to some expensive wiring problems. So I had to pray fervently that I wouldn't be pulled over, again. This was my custom every time I drove the dark country roads after a meeting: Pray favor with the police! At least the intensity kept me awake.

CORNELL UNIVERSITY (AGAIN)

14 HOURS LATER: After driving an hour, I was once again on Cornell University! It was a bright, sunny summer afternoon. This time I was speaking to a mixture of students and young ministers. I spoke for about sixty minutes. The fire and brashness was strong amid the passing by of secular college students. (We were in a tiny upper room on campus with small adobe-like windows and a rounded, short ceiling. There was no air-conditioning, and to me, it resembled a scene from the book of Acts.)

The strategies rolled, for impacting a culture through boldness and power. The call to recognize the state of emergency in our nation screamed! If we responded properly we could turn a country upside down. These young people were eating it up. They had the makings of modern day revivalists. After this we walked the campus and stood on strategic spots, releasing glory. One of which was over the place where the Satanic bible was kept many stories underground. One day, history will tell what was accomplished that afternoon.

GENEVEVA (AGAIN)

18 HOURS LATER: I arrived at the place where God introduced me to the "elephants". Many people came who had heard me speak, but also new faces were present. At the onset of this gathering, I helped lead worship for an hour, occasionally hitting my drum. (But I still refused "play it".)

When it was time to speak, the leader motioned for me to share, and then stepped out of the room. As I began to talk, a woman correcting me with her opinions, interrupted me. Then another woman chimed in. It went downhill from there. There were so many egos it was repugnant. Next, they tried to force a move of God. I sat there surveying the room thinking what a circus! Not only were they faking travail, but also there was no honor for me as the speaker. (I sensed this lack of respect was my unassuming nature, not to mention my youthful appearance.) Sigh. I was worn out from the past several weeks and did not have the patience to deal with this chaos. So I stood up to leave, but before I did I passed by the leader in the other room. She did not know what was happening in the main area because she had already released me.

"This is not God," I said to her. "I have no desire to participate. If this continues, I'm leaving."

She was calm and said, "What should I do?"

I asked, "Do you still want me to speak?"

She affirmed.

I said, "You're the leader, stop it."

So she did. You could have heard a pin drop. I then proceeded to share the message. I could tell instantly the fake travail may have left, but their dishonor for me remained intact. Righteous indignation was the only emotion I was capable of at this moment. Too much was at stake for our nation to play these stupid games. I opened my mouth and loosed the fire of God. And since I could discern their hearts, I started addressing their problems out loud. I told them to let go of their flesh and bad attitudes toward me. Some of them had bitterness and unforgiveness, "Let it go!" I yelled.

I said many, many hard things and rebuked them severely. I drove the point home that they were chosen by God to birth an awakening, and it was time they be about the Father's business! There was a revival well beneath their feet, they stood upon it everyday. "What are you doing with it!" I shouted.

Sniffles echoed throughout the room. Then wails began to occur. I refused to open my eyes because I didn't want to see cynicism. I kept preaching and preaching, releasing much reproof. Intercession broke out, and then travail hit. This time it was real. The power of God was everywhere. I finally opened my eyes to see some on the floor, some crying and some in utter shock. I went around the room and placed my hand on those who were seriously seeking God. This went on and on, until I knew I could leave. I walked out amidst prostrated souls and broken hearts. After I left, the meeting continued four more hours. I felt like I was experiencing a Finney story. The same manifestations, one hundred and fifty years later-- it was in the land.

That same day, the regional leader relayed an email had been sent from someone present, who didn't stay the entire time. Their life was radically affected! Another woman, who had traveled two hours to attend was transformed, too. All were utterly riveted by God's reviving fire. I'm sure there were quite a few testimonies of change, but I had to move on to the next city. Sadly, there was never time to hear the all feedback. (I had to trust it to the Lord, and keep my focus on the path ahead.)

CANANDAIGUA

20 HOURS LATER: Right after the crazy Geneva meeting, I shared with the intercessors of a church. There we sat, the few of us alone in a large sanctuary. I expounded on the vision for America and uncapping the wells. I told them they were the rudder for our nation. The key was long hours of uninterrupted worship and extended times of praying in tongues. Then we prayed in the spirit for quite some time. Our voices echoed throughout the sanctuary. Reams of power billowed out as we unabashedly cried in our heavenly languages. The leader wept, as she told me her spirit had yearned for this demonstration for years. She had known chartered out prayers mingled with worship were limiting to God.

That day, an ignition took place in the heart of a powerful, leading intercessor! She began to see a vision for her region and the different walks of life in which she was connected. A plan to possess land was resonating in her spirit, maybe even coming to life. Yes, Lord, let the bones rattle and the armies assemble!

7 DAYS ABLAZE FOR BATH

24 HOURS LATER: The past fourteen days had been very full since the prayer school in Bath. Now it was time for the follow-up seven nights of prayer. On this sunny afternoon, I met the owner of a yellow lake house and we toured what would be my home for the next week. (This woman and her husband turned out to be the finest people! Both of them were pillars, not only in their community but also in the Spirit.) When evening time arrived, I drove to downtown Bath. I parked my car on the street, near the place for intercession and walked hurriedly down the sidewalk. Suddenly my pace was arrested by the Lord's booming disclosure,

"If you don't play your drum you will be in disobedience."

Oh! I did not want to play that djembe! I loved it but I had no rhythm. I purposely left it in my backseat, and God was not going to let me get away with it. So I turned around and snatched it. When I finally entered the home, it was a full house; two living rooms filled with people, ready to pray. I scanned the faces, as I sat next to the regional leader. Within a few minutes, I launched the meeting. I commissioned everyone to pray in tongues. Then I sang and played the drum in a basic Native war beat; it was all I knew.

We prayed for the next two hours and it was fire from heaven! Afterwards, I was tired and drunk in the glory, but drove my typical late-night drive. This group of people prayed like no others I encountered. We did this for the next six days meeting in a different city every night. New people joined us each time. Pastors came. Leaders came. Those who worked in the marketplace came. Young people came. It was divine!

24 HOURS LATER: The second night we met on the outskirts of Bath at the regional leader's home. It too, was filled to capacity with people fervent in intercession!

SPENCERPORT

24 HOURS LATER: It was Wednesday, and the third night of

prayer for the Bath region. Unfortunately, I had to miss this session to drive a few hours to speak in Spencerport. As I pulled into the neighborhood, my brain could barely process anything, except wanting sleep. I remained parked in front of the house, worn out. The task of spreading the word to so many was taking its toll on me. Then out of the blue, a friend from Tulsa texted,

"For you, now."

I clicked on the link that followed and listened to the opening lines of a timely song. Rivers of tears trailed my cheeks.

"I hear the voice of one crying, 'Prepare the way of the Lord.'"

The words washed over my soul, bringing strength. I was reminded of my purpose and not to give up, even if I was faint. The fire reignited for a national awakening! I would not hold back but call forth the few attending that night to stand with me for their region. At that, I climbed out of my SUV and walked into the home group. About half of them had already heard the message, so I started playing my drum and singing. I could feel the ground in the area responding in the Spirit. I was encouraged, but it didn't take long to realize my fervency was solitary. I'm not sure those in attendance understood the urgency, or maybe they were expecting a sermon. Either way, I backed off from drumming and silenced my songs.

Afterwards, the leaders were honoring. But I sensed the group as a whole missed a moment of visitation. I drove another late night back for sleep, but I do not remember where. I do know, I didn't stay at the yellow lake house.

AVOCA

24 HOURS LATER: After a forty-five minute drive, I arrived at the fourth night of intercession for the Bath region. Some amazing worship leaders in the area hosted this meeting. The living room was packed out with new faces, even the adjacent room trailed with people. The custom was the same, pray in tongues for two

hours. This particular night when I played my drum, I hit a zone for the first time. It was as if Holy Spirit took over my hands. I heard rhythms, and knew how and where to place my hands on the djembe. During this process, I could feel and see an angel playing with me. The anointing was very, very thick.

As usual there were skeptics in the room who just came to check things out. They were not interested in prayer. In order to drown out their unbelief, the Lord told me to go around the room and place my hand on those who were serious. (I was to help them kick it up a few notches!) Several were left out. But breakthrough came.

LADY'S GROUP IN HORNELL

24 HOURS LATER: I was scheduled to speak at 9 a.m. at a weekly gathering that lasted until noon. I almost made it on time! Needless to say, it was quite a challenge for me to rise early and teach for a few hours. My body was fatigued, but I taught on intercession and many were encouraged. At the end of the meeting, the owner of the home railed against me.

This man was angry and offended because he didn't speak in tongues. He degraded me in front of the whole group for emphasizing this type of prayer. He claimed it was a gift like any other endowment, and that my speaking in tongues was no more important than his ability to play the keyboard! It was silly. After several bouts back and forth with this man, I simply replied Jesus didn't come to earth and suffer on a cross so we could have the gift of playing an instrument. He came so He could live inside of us. This truth silenced the man, but that didn't stop him from publicly demeaning me at two more meetings. I was growing tough skin!

CANISTEO

6 HOURS LATER: The fifth night of prayer was upon us and the city was Canisteo. I walked into a large church to see the congregation seats had been arranged into a gigantic circle. It spanned the entire sanctuary. There were tons of people and I was a bit overwhelmed. This was a prayer meeting, not a church

service. Why had so many shown up? This was not a rolling around, laughing kind of gathering. We were going sweat under the anointing, as we disciplined ourselves to pray in tongues for two hours!

At any rate, I sat down at the head of the circle. I was told there were several pastors in attendance. I scanned the room and thought; this is going to be interesting. I informed the people of my name and why I had come to New York. Then I said, "Pray in tongues." I led out over the microphone, playing my drum and singing songs of war and triumph. After about thirty minutes, the religious spirit from some of the pastors grew so strong, I felt I was being crushed. Why were they still here? If they didn't like it, they could leave. I couldn't figure out why they remained in the building since they were so agitated. I turned to the regional leader next me,

"I'm leaving, this is going no where. The religious spirit is horrible! They won't even pray."

I could tell she was not in agreement with me. So I reiterated,

"Either they leave, or I leave."

"Wait." She said. "Let's keep praying."

Out of honor for her, I agreed to stay. But, I thought, I'm not holding back one thing. I'll pray like I'm the only one in the room! And I did. For the next hour, the fire of God hit that place marvelously. People went into heavy travail. The power of God was electric. I sang in warring tongues and played the crap out of my drum. The land nearby that had been so defiled by the blood of slaughtered Native Americans was now cleansed. By the end of the prayer time, one, lone voice echoed in the sanctuary, and it was mine. The Presence was so thick no one else dared to speak.

When I closed the night out, a pastor approached me rapidly, asking I come to his church. I accepted. Another man approached me and invited me to a communist country (which will remain anonymous). He ran ministry schools there and I would always have an open door. He also shared he had a vision of the region while we prayed. It went back hundreds of years. He saw a Native American couple standing side-by-side holding hands and worshiping God. For the first time he watched the spiritual cleansing go all the way back to the beginning. What a testimony!

Two days after that, was a Sunday. The church that hosted the above meeting opened it doors like normal for the morning service, but it was not business as usual! The pastor began by addressing the congregation.

"Today," he said, "is going to be different."

He informed them they were old wineskins and he didn't want to miss out on what God had in store. He didn't want to be on the outside looking in. Also, there was an open microphone for members of the congregation to speak. A mighty upheaval happened that weekend. I'm sure that's only a fraction of the testimonies that occurred as a result of our fervent intercession. It was truly time to confront the fear of man.

I learned a mighty lesson that night. Sometimes the remedy to traditional, religious mentalities is simply to demonstrate the power of God. It was up to them to choose life and not remain in death. Some chose life that night. I can only hope they all left the death entrapment of churchiness.

HORNELL

24 HOURS LATER: Can you believe I found myself once again, at the man's house who was so venomous! This night was a time of discussion, because the people had grown so much in prayer, divine strategy was needed. Many stories were shared concerning the positive effects the prayer school and the nights of intercession had had on the communities. So I introduced some new revelation that was quite profound. But it certainly wasn't a time to gloat; the angry man made sure of it, this last attack was the greatest of them all.

The entire room watched as he verbally pummeled me. No one stood up for my help, so I went toe-to-toe with the man. I stated my case and refused to back down. I felt a bit like the apostle Paul when the bible says he was arguing in the synagogue daily! The evening closed on a stern note, because I refused to renounce my stance. Soon apologies came from observers who did not stop his vehemence. Like Paul, I shook the serpent off into the fire.

CORNING

24 HOURS LATER: I arrived to another packed-out house with lots of excitement. After explaining the vision to the newcomers, I started praying in tongues while playing the djembe. By now, I had learned to release a resonance that penetrated many realms. But this night a challenge arose in the area of sound.

You see, someone else had a hand drum and was playing too. The problem was the spirit behind the rhythms was wrong. Clearly, the individual was trying to conjure up Native American authority from the ground through the drum. It was strange fire, meaning: it wasn't worship to God but it was idolatry. It was the placing of one's identity in an expression. I was frustrated, not knowing what to do since this person was a Christian!

Trying to explain would make me sound crazy. So I decided to take the easy way out and stop playing; hopefully the other person would stop too. It worked, but only temporarily. When I began to drum again, they did as well! The false anointing was filling the room and clashing with the true intercession.

Befuddled, I leaned over to the regional leader and asked if she sensed "new age". She confirmed. I stopped the meeting and addressed the issue, as God was whispering in my ear about the fear of the Lord. I did it diplomatically, by not calling out the individual. I stated in a general sense that it was dangerous to try and tap a native sound from the ground; this opens the door for a wrong spirit. Immediately, offense was taken and the person defended themselves openly, bringing exposure.

The group was confused, and then I had no choice but to explain. My drum sound was indigenous. I wasn't trying to conjure up something. I was praising the Lord as it says in the bible. In the midst of my explanation, the person did not want to admit what they were doing and left the room. (I'm sure roots of insecurity and rejection were the cause of these actions. Unknowingly, a door had been opened to a false spirit, by aligning the personal identity with something other than God.)

So we concluded the night of prayer in the spirit of intensity! A few were quite upset with me and talk began in the community. Soon a split occurred because I exposed what many knew was wrong, but could not explain. The division needed to occur until repentance emerged. We cannot mix truth and error, and then expect God to bless us.

Many things happened in this region as a result of the prayer school and nights of intercession. It would take way too much space in this book to tell of the ripple effects and lives that were altered. But the ministries that were affected or launched were impressive! Here are a few. The regional leader was infused with a fire and energy during the impartation time of the school. The Lord told her to run. So she lapped the room. This prophetic act launched her into a new season. She reiterated how her processes changed when I placed my hand on her head. (Like a metamorphosis.)

Another apostolic couple followed God's commissioning for continual prayer by launching a group on Mondays. Then, those nights of prayer moved them right into the next season of starting a church in downtown. It grew very quickly. Now, this dynamic duo pretty much birthed twins, as they also launched a home group just over the border in Pennsylvania. It too, quickly expanded. Some young adults were being delivered from addictions and receiving the baptism of the Holy Spirit.

A year and a half later I was talking to the regional leader who told me they were experiencing nothing but breakthrough. The follow-through in this community was astounding. They took seriously the revelations I taught, and applied them exactly. And because my words were not my own, what they did prospered!

6

APRIL CONTINUES

FREEVILLE

36 HOURS LATER: I was to speak twice in one day, two hours in the afternoon and a few in the evening. The church was bright, beautiful and very new. The people came from different locations. In the afternoon session, I spoke on the revelations God was giving me for the nation, especially concerning boldness and rejecting the fear of man. I told personal stories of power evangelism. The accounts were quite sobering. Then we broke for dinner and the pastor told me he was challenged, in a good way! What great character he and his family exuded. If the leaders in the rest of the nation had their amazing attitudes, our culture would surely be rocked.

After dinner, it was time for the evening service. We decided to pray for 2 hours, Tracey-style! There were many in attendance and it was awesome. The congregation was on fire. Many were pacing the large space in the back, and several gathered in the front, some sat in seats while others knelt. But everyone was focused solely on tapping the heart of God for the area. As was my custom, I sat on the front row with my back to the audience, and my hand drum between my knees. I prayed in tongues over the microphone, and sang songs of war and triumph. The whole valley opened up before my spiritual sight, I could see and feel the shifting of the ground with each thud of the djembe. (One leader present described the sound as "spiritual fracking", which brings up a point. When I played my djembe it did not sound like a fast, high-pitched conga. It had a very loose skin, so the sound was deep and riveting, like a native war drum.)

Anyway, the power was undeniable. Many times I was doubled-over in dry heaves from the divine cleansing taking place. Even the pastor grabbed a drum and began to play in unison. We were a spiritual troop enforcing the kingdom of God through worship and prayer. After we finished, the atmosphere was tangibly pure and very quiet. When we were all silent, then the pastor commented how interesting it was to see the high place we had attained. The mystery was shrouded until we were still enough to recognize it!

CANANDAIGUA

36 HOURS LATER: I re-visited another centralized New York city. It was a small home group near Canandaigua. The little living room was packed out. When I walked in, all my sensors were sensing to say the least! I could tell before I reached the kitchen for coffee they were not accustomed to prayer. Nevertheless, when the time came to speak, I shared the vision for intercession and America.

My customary two-hour, fiery prayer session quickly turned into five minutes of speaking in tongues. Regardless, the young woman sitting next to me was rocked. She was crying and crying how she had given up her gift of intercession; that night she felt the fire again! She went on telling stories, reminding herself she *did* have seeds of fervency within her being. Another woman across the room was greatly blessed and being counseled by another leader present. After it was all said and done, I thought to myself, if the only reason I came was to reignite one intercessor, it was well worth the drive.

SYRACUSE PRAYER SCHOOL

12 HOURS LATER: It was the morning after the monumental, five-minute prayer session, and it was early. I was barely awake when I heard the sound of a sword being ripped from its sheath. It shook me to the core, as it was right in front of my face! Instantly, came a word of knowledge: I would encounter a religious spirit that night, and this sword was the granted authority to shred it to pieces.

8 HOURS LATER: I drove an hour to Syracuse to meet the leaders for a nice dinner. I had never encountered them, so this was our introduction. I was quiet through most of the meal, and then afterwards, we headed to the church for the evening session of the prayer school. On the way I grew very anxious, and for a couple of reasons. One, the dinner conversation revealed why I had heard an unsheathing sword; I would have to sever a spirit before I could teach without restraint. Two, I was eager to learn about a name on an email the leader had sent me that morning. It was the man's name I heard in the spirit several months prior!

So, when I arrived at the church I approached the leader. I asked him about the person in the email, and then displayed my phone with the same name and dated document. He looked blankly at me, and said the man was from Massachusetts. Then he rattled off several accompanying titles and walked off. He was not too impressed. So I dropped it.

Five minutes later, it was time for the meeting. But after half an hour of preliminaries, (that I did not know were scheduled) I was given the service. So, with my djembe in one hand and a microphone in the other, I walked up the stairs of the stage and sat down on the second step, front and center. I said nothing and didn't even look up. I placed the drum between my knees and put the microphone up close; I hit it once. The sound was deep and riveting. I did it again. I repeated this for a few minutes. Then I stood up with my eyes closed. (You could have heard a pin drop!)

Breaking the silence, I unsheathed the sword. I started addressing religious spirits and demons in other tongues over the microphone. (The religious ones were on the people. The evil spirits were the larger entities over the region that knew I was in town). I did this for about ten minutes. It was loud, abrupt and authoritative. Then, I rolled out the interpretation in English. The words were so strong, I expected to be ushered off the stage and asked to leave. But when I finished and opened my eyes, everyone was in shock; no one spoke or moved. The fear of the Lord was everywhere. Then I started teaching.

What I said was well received and there was very little resistance, because of how I began. You see, I knew by the Spirit of God who did not honor me. And I knew intimidation toward me through pride would be the hindrance. So I dealt with all of that when I was speaking in tongues. I knew exactly what I was saying, when I was saying it. Therefore, when I spoke out the interpretation in English, it was toward the people in the room who would try to hinder me, and to the principalities watching the meeting.

After the Friday evening teaching, I received a forwarded text from one of the attendees. He could not make it for the Saturday session, as he had to work through the night. It read:

"I've been praying at least half the night in the Spirit, at work. I have never done that before, it's crazy! Something happened to me! It's good. Take good notes and ask her to pray for me, that God would really open this up for me..."

12 HOURS LATER: It was time for the all-day session for Syracuse! It was an early morning for me as usual because I remained sleep deprived, but I was looking forward it. I would teach and impart for five hours. After the morning session we broke for lunch and many people came to the podium to talk to me. One woman pressed through and was approaching quickly. She had a crazed look in her eye.

The Lord said, "Get away from her!" I backed away very fast, when she yelled, "Where are you going for lunch!"

Instantly, the impression came that if this woman had a gun in her purse she would me find me and shoot me. A leader quickly stepped in between her and I; he grabbed my arm and walked me away. At lunch I told the facilitators my suspicion of the woman. I felt odd telling them, but I sensed she was a real threat to me. They commented how they had never seen her before.

When we arrived back at the church for the afternoon session. I was put in a back room until the people were seated. This prevented me from being rushed by everyone. As I sat waiting, I was battling fear. I decided to war on my drum and paralyze any evil spirits in the atmosphere. It worked. Eventually, I was brought out, and the sessions continued. I was thankful these leaders understood higher spiritual levels. This made the effect of the school that much more powerful.

During the afternoon session, I was acutely aware this school in particular would have a significant effect on the Syracuse area. The words and revelations were shaking realms and societies well beyond the sanctuary. I made mention of a Syracuse University several times. I felt there would be a move of God there. Then I asked if there was one nearby, and everyone laughed! I wasn't aware of one, but my spirit could see it, as I scanned the region.

Also, I was told the central location for the original government in America, (before the white man came) was in Syracuse. The Iroquois had established it. I learned our system of democracy was taken primarily from the way Native Americans had structured their land. I bet you don't hear that much! At the end of the prayer school, I anointed everyone with oil and asked all present to speak in tongues. I requested they forego all chitchat in the room. This was a powerful time of prayer and it lasted a while.

Finally, I sat on the steps of the stage with the leader near me. The whole group went silent. Holiness was everywhere and so was the Fear of the Lord. We could not close the meeting. Everyone was afraid to move or talk, so I was handed the microphone. I closed. Then the leader leaned over, and through a broken voice said he had seen the angels that were with Lot in Sodom and Gomorrah.

"We've bought a little more time." He added.

I felt it in my bones. I knew God was heeding our prayers and staying destruction so America could have a chance to repent. The rudder was doing its job!

SYRACUSE PRAYER DRIVE

4 DAYS LATER: I drove an hour for lunch with some wonderful Pastors in Syracuse. After we finished, the wife and I decided to go for a prayer drive in the darkest parts of the city. I took my drum and played it in the front seat! We drove to a few parking lots, pornographic businesses, shady restaurants and apartments buildings. This woman was bold, and even drove up front and center, while someone was exiting one of the establishments. Of course we were praying in tongues!

ITHACA PRAYER SCHOOL

24 HOURS LATER: Ithaca, home of Cornell University! Beautiful, and liberal. I arrived on a sunny, Friday evening. The host church pastor was there early, ready and worshiping. I taught for two hours to a large group of hungry intercessors. People came from a variety of places. Then we convened back the next morning for four more hours of teaching and one hour of impartation.

At the end of this school, I prayed for the sick. And I stepped into a glory realm I had not known. It felt like a bubble around me. It was easy to pray for the people, like I didn't have to believe, but merely speak, because Jesus was so present. At the front of the line, an evil spirit came out of someone with a mere whisper. I don't know the majority of the results, I was too exhausted to ask. I'm sure more than one person was healed. One lady in particular had a crippling disease, I prayed over her extensively and my hands were hot like fire. I saw nothing outwardly, but she felt some effect in her body. Often times people just walk out of sickness after prayer. So I left it to the Lord. I wished I had remembered to pray for the sick in the other schools.

I walked out that afternoon physically wiped out and very, very drunk with the glory of God. I could barely function in the natural. I drove to a large parking lot nearby, and sat in my SUV in the sun. I had a couple of hours to recoup before my next speaking engagement.

CORNELL UNIVERSITY

3 HOURS LATER: I was back on the campus to teach at a weekly gathering for the students. It started at 7 p.m. Most of those present were Christians, some were not. A few were deep with the Lord. My subject for the night was how God scattered the languages of man back in Genesis but reunited them through the baptism of the Holy Spirit. We could all speak the same language now; God's language, if we received it!

I prayed over a few students when I finished teaching, one young Asian man was really touched. Another young lady of Indian decent approached me and expressed her astonishment at the revelation. Most of the students were from other countries and I was told the fruit of what I did might not be seen for years to come. That seemed to be my life story! Stay hidden, plow ground, plant seeds and rejoice in my intimacy with God.

I left the campus about 10 p.m. I needed to be alone after such an intense outflow of the anointing, so I decided to stay in a hotel, rather than in my host home. The only problem: the accommodations were all full. So I reconnected with my host, saying I would I arrive shortly. When I knocked on the front door, no one heard me. I texted again, no response. So I continued calling other places, until I found a vacancy, in another city!

On my way to the hotel, I passed through a college party town and it was midnight, so naturally I was pulled over for my buzzed out tail light. I was utterly exhausted but thankful the officer let me go. I arrived safe and secure in my hotel at 1 a.m. I was so tired I could not sleep. Check out was in ten hours, and I needed to rest up, for the next day would begin five days of intercession for the Ithaca region.

After this school, there was only enough time for five days of follow-up prayer, as my schedule was booked. But it was no less effective! The intercession times in Ithaca would prove to be some of the most intense encounters. These meetings were large and the people were spiritually mature. Not to mention the regional leader had been crying out for revival for *decades*. I stepped into a spiritual heritage and upon a strong foundation. It felt like I was spring boarding into supernatural manifestations of God.

5 DAYS ABLAZE FOR ITHACA

19 HOURS LATER: Night number one. I was back in Freeville! It was the same church with the pastors of great character. I was glad to revisit. We did our usual two hours of praying in tongues while I beat my drum. Again, the open sanctuary was littered with people sitting, standing, pacing, or on the floor. I sat on the front row with my eyes shut, concentrating on the spirit realm, as I prayed over the microphone. I also handed it off to other leaders in the room to speak over the region.

My voice was starting go after the months of intercession. I had forgotten to warm it up several cities prior and it affected my vocal chords. I remembered what a minister told me back in Toledo. She said if you ever lose your voice eat a spoonful of honey. Now I carried with me a Mac, a drum, a bible and jar of honey!

CORNELL UNIVERSITY

24 HOURS LATER: I walked across a long parking lot, and through pretty, green grass to arrive at a campus building. On the second floor in one of the rooms, we would pray for two hours in tongues. And I was a little nervous; my mind was playing tricks on me. I kept rehearsing all of the hate-speech laws in America. My thoughts: this is a liberal school. I am going to pray *in tongues* and *in the name of Jesus* over a microphone inside of a classroom! I'm not a student, what if I stir up so many demons that I get arrested.

It was not probable, but in my mind it was highly plausible. I resolved within myself to pray with so much authority that it would bind the devil, not stir him up. I guess it worked nobody was attained. Ha-ha! On a serious note, halfway though the prayer session I stepped out into the hall. A student happened to be walking by the room, obviously gripped by the sensation in the atmosphere. (The glory was extremely tangible.) He stared with huge eyes and a shocked look as he passed the door. He turned back several times, glaring intently.

FREEVILLE- RECORDING STUDIO

24 HOURS LATER: This was the third night of intercession for Ithaca. We prayed in a tiny studio. The acoustics were great for my drum, although it probably deafened everyone else. This was a smaller meeting, but very effective. Afterwards, I was handed a business card from a man who was involved in college ministry in the Auburn area. If I came that way he was interested in working with me. That night, I drove an hour back to a host home. Midnight seemed to be my unwritten curfew and once again, it took a while to unwind. But no matter the depths of my weariness, I kept the same schedule- up with the sun. This helped me avoid body jet lag.

FREEVILLE- CHURCH OF THE REVIVAL

24 HOURS LATER: This night stands out to me for some reason. We met in a large room with concrete floors, wooden beams and a very tall ceiling. It was an aged church, but it felt like a historic barn. Many moons ago, a revival broke out there. So I'm sure we walked in and upon that foundation. People came from all over the region to join in prayer.

As customary to the meetings I held across New York, many of the attendees did not know each other. They were mostly leaders from different churches, cultures, races and cities. But unity is a beautiful thing! This night probably forty attended. There was a large circle of chairs in which we sat, but that didn't last long. Soon the whole company was pacing, engaged intensely and praying in tongues.

All prayed for the duration, (roughly an hour and a half) and afterwards, we did a de-briefing. It was amazing to hear how God used each person to pray breakthrough. Some prayed for the city, some for the university and others for Washington D.C. or the government. Innumerable topics were covered, but all prayed in tongues without stopping. Every prayer was effective. We were interceding according to the Spirit of God. He was intervening through us.

This type of intercession was definitely new to the prayer culture of America. It seemed so many were accustomed to constant interaction with each other or prayer lists, that they forgot to tap the deeper realms through extensive praying in tongues. But God was raising up a new breed of warriors who would go the distance!

ITHACA- THE OUTSKIRTS

24 HOURS LATER: It was the end of the intercession days for Ithaca and I was ready to close out in victory. As I pulled into the parking lot, I sensed it. Something was not right. I wondered what would unfold! I parked my car and quickly grabbed my drum. I headed for the main door of the building. Peaceful worship greeted me, so far so good! I approached the front of the room where a microphone was set up for me. I sat down and caught everyone up to speed who had not attended the other prayer sessions. Then I struck my drum as usual, to set the atmosphere.

As I began singing, I could tell many were not on the same page. I detected a religious force manifesting through someone. Quite honestly, there was no spirit of prayer upon half of them. I wondered why some of them came. I mean I was glad, sort of, but why come to a prayer meeting to sleep or stare at a wall.

I overlooked the lack of desire and focused on praying for the region, myself. (I remembered what I learned in Bath.) I sang and spoke in tongues for an hour, along with the few who were on board, but to no avail. We could not "get out of the room". For some reason, the people weren't willing. I sensed disdain toward me. I suspected this was the hindrance impeding our ability to join hearts. I was faced with a decision. We couldn't keep pretending we were in unity when we were not. The situation needed to be addressed; this was part of my job description, and cleaning the rudder is a gritty task!

I pulled the prayer leader aside and asked what she was discerning. She said there were two different camps in the room. Some didn't like the way I was praying and thought I was new-age. I almost laughed out loud. She suggested I not play my drum. I declined. I was not going to bow to a religious spirit and compromise the assignment the Lord had given me. The prayer leader gave me permission to address the people. So I walked back up the aisle and sat down in my chair at the front. I leaned over the microphone,

"Okay, everyone can stop now."

A hush fell. Faces stared. I proceeded, "We can't get out of this room because you have issues with me. You don't like the way I pray and some of you think I'm new-age. I don't have a history of new age, I was never involved in it, and I don't know anything about it."

I continued, "This is voluntary. If you don't like it, you can leave, but know these attitudes are what is wrong with America."

I proceeded to close the service, "I can't pray anymore because you won't honor me. There's no point in continuing."

One lady piped up, "This is the spirit in Ithaca you are dealing with."

I said, "No it's not. I can handle that no problem. It's the people in this room. You all don't like me and because we aren't in unity, there is no reason to continue."

I said all of this very calm and was not upset or angry in the slightest. I wanted them to see the petty issues in our Christian cultures and how they effect the manifestation of God's power. Too many leaders are afraid to confront problems. I was not; I knew our nation was at stake. If God's people refused to catch the fire we were in trouble. Then, Another lady spoke up, "What do you suggest we do?"

I replied, "First, get rid of your offense against me. Forgive me. Whatever problem you have; let it go. I don't have a problem with any of you, but your hearts need to be right towards me."

Another lady piped up, she had plugged her ears because the drum was loud to her. She explained this is why she moved to the lobby. I told her location was irrelevant, what matters is the heart. If the heart is right the prayer will be tangibly fervent. The book of James reveals this concept. Another man commented the Holy Spirit was looking for a place to land in the room but couldn't find one. To me, this summed it up. God was willing to co-labor with us as we released His presence over Ithaca, but some of the people would not open their hearts. There was nothing I could do about it.

After the discussion, the allotted two hours was up. I was fine with it and at peace with the people. I knew God was using me to expose some root issues so they could be more effective in the long run. I turned to the pastor present and asked what he had to say. He was kind and released me, saying it was now between he and the people to seek God together. They would find the source of the problem. I walked to my car, and a man offered to carry my drum. When we reached my driver's door, he handed over my instrument of war and said, "You're a gutsy lady."

LAKEHOUSE WOMEN'S RETREAT

24 HOURS LATER: The lake house was beautiful but this was not a retreat of comfort and ease! It was a war-room gathering, per the one who rallied the ladies. She was the strategic leader I met from Niagara Falls back in February. She had scheduled this months ago, and was revved up to bring her intercessors from two hours away. Many came and we started the first night talking on the cost of being a warrior. I shared stories of Navy SEALs, Olympic champions and even the hard-nosed mentality of General Patton. The women seemed to eat it up.

"This is not prayer as usual," I told them. "It's warrior-praying! It's heart-felt intercession."

There is nothing easy about it, in the sense that it will cost us everything. It will cost us the privilege of walking in the flesh. It requires we live disciplined lives, separating ourselves from the filth of the world. It demands we learn to keep our minds focused while interceding, so that we can be effective. It's a different mentality all together. It isn't appeasing, man pleasing, idolatrous or shy in nature. It is fervent, intense, on-purpose, non-compromising and powerful in delivery, producing change!

THE EXAMPLES

Navy SEALs are good at what they do because they live a cut above the rest. They have many attributes, but their discretion and humility keep them alive! Too many intercessors crave recognition these days. Self-centeredness must be axed, and inner healing is of utmost importance. Without these preeminent objectives, don't bother picking up the mantle to pray.

George Patton helped defeat the Nazi's because he was relentless in his pursuit. He had no stop button! That, mixed with his positive, no option but winning mentality, kept the army alert and moving forward. Not enough people travail until the victory comes. This is because faith and vision for triumph are absent. In order to see the desired result, there must be a clear goal and pressure must be applied to press through to the conclusion.

Olympic champions know the cost to go for the gold! Long, long hours, days and years dedicated to achieving their purpose is what they sacrifice. Not to mention pleasant food, fun and what many call a normal life. But they are driven to be a contender on the world's stage, and in the end, it is worth every moment of surrender!

12 HOURS LATER: The next morning I arrived to beautiful view of a sunny lake. I shared more on the heart of intercession, discerning God's voice, prayer room etiquette and many more

topics until we broke for the afternoon. I told them in order to properly discern God's voice we must eradicate the negative distractions that so permeate our daily lives. I listed out many things, culturally speaking. Also, I made clear that once we create these voids, they should be replaced with lots of quality time with God. The more concentrated hours spent with Him, the easier it will be to detect His voice and leadings. Many things about this topic I broke down in their hearing.

I also shared extensively about the behavior that should accompany intercessors when they are praying in corporate settings. For instance, fake travail, praying loudly in the flesh to get attention, and leaders who refuse to confront the flaky conduct. Neither did I leave out how to humbly enter a prayer meeting, or how to properly administrate one so that a leader isn't leading, but Holy Spirit is governing. I continued until all the topics for that session were covered.

6 HOURS LATER: Many women were hungry, but a few seemed smug. I suspected some ego issues, such as competition and jealousy. But I wasn't completely sure. I overlooked these nuances at first, until the third day, and then something had to be done.

12 HOURS LATER: It was the last morning of the retreat and I walked into the room with a Holy Spirit impression, "Someone has undone what I have taught through their words." I brushed it off and started to teach, but the attitudes on some of the ladies were still not pleasant. Again I thought, why were they here if they didn't like me or agree with what I was teaching? So, once more, I pulled the nearest leader aside and asked what she was sensing.

Her words confirmed all I was seeing. She also mentioned that a minister at the retreat spoke to the group before I arrived, but she was unaware of the topic. I sighed and shook my head, walking back down the hall. When I re-entered the room, I bottom-lined the people. I knew most were on board. But I was trying to push the few that were not to a place of breaking; hoping they would either repent, or dismiss themselves.

(I was training warriors and good generals are not patsies! My younger brother didn't label me Patton for nothin'.)

First, I made sure they knew the retreat was voluntary. I told them they were welcome to leave if they so desired. No one moved. I reiterated my predicament, "I can not teach as long as you are warring against me with your human spirit."

Again, no one admitted to hard feelings. So, I pressed through the rest of the afternoon and wrestled the judgment against me the entire session. Secretly, I wished whoever was upset would have left, because I wanted to be effective. I knew Gideon's army was whittled down until it could be successful! This is a principle overlooked by church leaders who are "building a ministry". They go after numbers and fail to understand God's thoughts are not our thoughts, and His ways are higher than our ways.

When we closed-out the retreat, I stood outside talking with the leader. Another minister brought up the topic of "coverings". She said she did not have free reign to pray the way she needed to when attending her church. It was quite a dilemma. I exhorted her strongly out of love for her future, asking why she even bothered to go. (I knew people like that wouldn't stand in the heat of a battle. First sign of trouble or persecution and they're hittin' the road Jack!)

"You better be able to pray with power! Your life might depend on it!" I raised my voice. The words echoed.

I reiterated, "Your life! And the lives of others!"

We parted ways and I hoped to keep them as friends. But mostly I hoped they understood the urgency of the hour. There was a cost to triumph under enemy fire. My point was that our deliverance comes from God. Permission to release prevailing prayer does not come from any human. Those held in the confines of church positioning rather than God's kingdom order have no backbone! Why would anyone put themselves under that false protection. It's like standing under a screen in a rainstorm thinking you won't get wet. The religious mentalities that operate by "permission from man" are full of holes! They have no real substance to them. And they certainly have no ability to protect.

WNY

I was told that out of this retreat a few ladies launched a recurring, regional prayer gathering at a home in Orchard Park. Many attended, and all ages too!

THE OSWEGO CONNECTION

3 DAYS LATER: I received a mass email from the Syracuse leader about a worship event in Oswego. A man on the list replied back to him saying he felt compelled to drive five and a half hours from Massachusetts; there was some connection he needed to make. The reply wasn't necessarily unusual, except the man had the same name I heard in the spirit back in February. The Syracuse leader remembered I had mentioned it in April when I showed him my phone, but he didn't know what to make of it. So if I came, the instructions were a promised introduction. Needless to say, I could not wait!

I made the hour and fifteen-minute drive and arrived at a church with tons of people. I sat near the back and enjoyed blending in with the crowd. I had been there half an hour when Mr. Massachusetts was escorted back to meet me. I proceeded to tell him I had heard his name in the spirit in February. I held up the document on my phone, untouched and dated.

He looked blankly at me and said, "That's me." I said, "I know."

Then he walked off. I was a baffled. (I drove over an hour for this?) He quickly turned around and shook my hand, saying it was nice to meet me. That was it; he went back to his seat. The service continued another hour and a half. I wanted so bad to leave and go to sleep, but the mystery got the best of me. I thought there has to be more to this story. So, I waited and waited, and a few people recognized me, so we were talking. I was also meeting new faces.

Then just about the time I was ready to leave, the Syracuse leader's wife asked if I had met the Massachusetts man. I told her I had. She then proceeded to walk me toward him. As I approached him I was nervous as to why he blew me off. But I struck up a conversation anyway. He didn't seem too interested, so he started stacking chairs and talking,

"God told me the wells of the *first* great awakening with Jonathon Edwards and John Wesley would be uncapped through intercession." Bam, bam, bam! The chairs were being slammed together quickly. I just stared at him.

Then, he rattled off the geographical locations of the wells and the heritage along with them. He said many things about those matters and I was almost speechless. Then, he told me of his ministry to street people, and ended with his miraculous testimony. I was blown away. I responded very nervously,

"Sir, I believe I need to tell you some things."

Bam, bam, bam! He looked up from stacking his chairs, "Well, I guess you listened to my spill. I can listen to yours."

With that, we sat down and I started talking. I told him I had been on the road six months, and one day last fall when I was driving God said to me:

"A prayer initiative to turn a nation; a strategy to awaken a nation that has gone dry; but it's not really dry. There are wells beneath the ground that must be re-awakened and tapped. Holiness is a part of this land; it is a heritage for this people. You will call them back to their purpose and re-establish or re-put the vision before them- the American people. There will be a response far and wide, as many will be saved and restored. The great revival that has been prophesied is about to manifest. People are ready and they are hungry."

Then I continued, "God told me worshipers and intercessors are the rudder for the nation. It is not the politicians that will turn

America. Worshipers and intercessors are going to create the atmosphere conducive for climatic change in cities of America. Without them change will not occur! They control the waves, what they say goes! The initiative is to gather the musicians and intercessors for an all out onslaught of glory in the Spirit."

I continued still, "I have been in New York for nearly six months. I stood on Finney's grave on the way into New York and unbeknownst to me, he was the one who led the second great awakening. God has given me the task of uncapping that well. So when you said what you did about the first great awakening I was taken back. I have been holding prayer schools all over, teaching and igniting intercession to birth a third great awakening in America. I don't know why I heard your name in the spirit, but I think there is a reason we have met."

At this point I had his undivided attention. He said, "Tracey, I drove five and a half hours to be here. I had a small encounter with God in the car but that is not why I'm here. I'm here to meet you."

Then he rattled off some statistics, "I am a leader at the largest (certain) denominational church in the northeast. Our city is home to the largest witches coven in North America, 2,300 witches. We have anywhere from sixteen to twenty-three witches attend our services every Sunday. We talked to the leader of this coven who revealed how they pray against us. They do not want us to meet in church buildings and pray in large corporate gatherings. My pastor is a Mason."

He looked right at me and said, "Tracey, we need you."

There was a long pause of silence. I couldn't believe what I was hearing. I envisioned myself entering the territory alone and playing my drum, while warring in tongues over the region. I thought what incredible warfare for one person! If I hadn't heard his name in the spirit I would not have signed up for this one. Nevertheless, we exchanged information and the date for the prayer school was soon set. It would be the end of June.

WELLSVILLE PRAYER SCHOOL

48 HOURS LATER: To recap the fifteen days leading up to Wellsville: I completed the two-day Ithaca prayer school, followed by five nights of intercession in various surrounding towns. I also did a strategic daytime meeting in yet an additional city, as well as a the three-day retreat at the lake house in Geneva, finalized by the meeting in Oswego.

Now, I had arrived in Wellsville. This was to be another weekend prayer school. The pastor who invited me was present in a prayer meeting a month prior, and he had such a humble spirit. Before I confirmed the dates with him the Lord showed me his face, blazing with brokenness for revival. (New York is truly the land of awakening; it's just a matter of time before the whole nation experiences the repercussions.)

This particular weekend seemed to be overflowing with revelation. Not only had God given me more, but also the people were desperate and pulling virtue from my spirit. I remember thinking I could have continued for hours but physical strength was lacking. We ended on a Saturday afternoon and I traveled an hour to the yellow lake house to rest. I was scheduled to drive all day on Monday to Toledo so I could speak Tuesday night, and then drive to Oklahoma on Thursday.

7

THE HUMAN SPIRIT

During my journey I discovered so many things about the human spirit, I could probably write a dozen books! Mostly, I learned dependence on the Lord. He truly became my best friend, my husband, my mother, my father; my everything. I drew strength from Him. I learned to live in the impossible and do what others said couldn't be done. Although these were irreplaceable attributes, I was absolutely exhausted at this stage of the trip and counting the days until my one-year was finished. Six months remained but it felt more like a decade. Even though my assignment was extreme, the spiritual terrain was not out of my jurisdiction. It was the human side of things that nearly took me out!

I spent many afternoons sitting in my SUV crying from weariness and loneliness. I was forlorn because I found no camaraderie in my field of labor; so maintaining emotional stability was a constant challenge. If I had known someone who comprehended the task I was undertaking it would have helped immensely. But I didn't and my heart ached. So I did my best to confide in the people I did know. Unfortunately their conversations always turned selfish, toward their own struggles. The result: their self-interest drove me to silence and further isolation, unless I was ministering corporately. Obviously, I was viewed as a commodity; a solution for the spiritual drought everyone was facing. And I remember it oh, so clearly. The pull from the people left me so depleted, I could barely think or speak at times. Not to mention the draw from the land, it was insanely parched.

HEAR YE

Being an apostolic, single woman is not for sissies! I'm convinced the rare combination of being unmarried at forty, and without children or a home base is why so many challenges emerged. And thinking on these things only added to my loneliness. I never felt like I fit, no matter where I went. I mean, the only ones in my shoes were twenty years my junior, and I had way too much life experience for them to remotely relate.

Of course there were people my own age, but they were consumed with rearing children, cooking, keeping house and wage earning. I could not relate to them! There was such a gap, as their lifestyle distracted my focus. It's not that I didn't desire a "normal" life but God had a different plan for me. So being on the road and fulfilling my purpose was exhilarating, I just wished for companions my age with the same passions.

MISUNDERSTANDING

As I traveled, many didn't understand my predicament, and they often expressed what I should or should not do. My mode of operation made absolutely no sense to the natural man. Only through the eyes of Holy Spirit could my arrangement be understood. (I'm speaking of my spiritual endowments here.) You see, I am an "atmospheres" person and my gifts are mostly stratospheric. Meaning, my turf is in the heavenlies and the unseen realm. So, not only was God using me to uncap wells of revival, He had sent me to displace territorial spirits through intercession, and my mere presence. Just the same, He was unlocking many leaders' potential. I was His gateway. It was rewarding, but taxing, and this is what evaded comprehension. People often informed me

I shouldn't travel by myself. (We already know I didn't want to be alone!) But I couldn't be effective with a team who was clueless to the realm in which God had positioned me?

This was a pioneering work. It took an incredible amount of focus and sensitivity to Holy Spirit to do it successfully. The weight of carrying an inexperienced individual, along with the assignment would have crushed me. Plus, I had no finances to support another person's bills, food and lodging. I was doing good to keep up with myself!

DRAINS AND MENTALITIES

Even more frustrating were the innocent but traditional mentalities. A few people wanted to know what was my website, and then others inquired about "my" ministry. For some reason, both agitated my spirit. And the few who inquired about my "covering" or suggested I "get" one, rubbed me the wrong way for sure! Were these people serious? Did they have an inkling of what was going on in America? We didn't have time to decorate pretty websites or sport frou-frou ministries. I spent my days alone processing in heavenly places with strategies from the Lord. I could care less about websites or TV, or the news for that matter! And I didn't need a "covering" capping me off spiritually or telling me what to do. (That was God's job.)

Another significant drain to my soul involved those attending the schools. They expected me to take their personal, prayer requests, as if *I* was responsible for them since I was teaching on prayer. Finally, I conveyed I came to give fishing poles, not cooked fish! This offended some, while others were pushed into higher levels. They were forced to draw on God's Spirit and not mine.

Eventually, this stopped. But what didn't stop was others tapping my strength in a different way. (Now, the people weren't solely to blame. Some of these problems originated from clergymen, they are the ones responsible for creating a culture of dependence. These ministers actually want people to be reliant upon them. So when someone like myself comes along and doesn't desire a following, the people don't know what to do; it's a new concept for them.)

Anyway, after a prayer school or an intercession time, a heavy anointing rested upon me and the people would flood the pulpit to tell stories. Many would stand there for long periods, seemingly mesmerized. This affected me greatly. I was exhausted and needed to lie down before I fell down, but they didn't care. They wanted what they wanted. I asked the Lord why this was so draining since I loved people and wanted to hear feedback. He said they were captivated with the anointing, and were not so much concerned about telling stories, as they liked the "feel good" around me. This was a horrible experience! And my body suffered. I now felt bad for judging other ministers who left directly after services. There's only so much a person can handle.

I finally informed those who had questions, comments, and stories or demanded I talk to them right then, to send an email. I never received the emails! Only a few people on my entire trip ever inquired over the Internet. They weren't interested in something that would cost them. They wanted the "feel good" and an easy way out. To me this provided another key to why the prayer movement in America needed such an overhaul. The "superstar" mentality was alive and well. But we need an army, not a hierarchy.

LEADERSHIP AGENDAS

Okay, I would be amiss if I didn't share the issues I experienced with leadership along the way. I'll tell you right off the bat; I'm sharing these things for a couple of reasons. One, so you'll better have a grip on what it was like day in and day out for me. And two, to expose the hindrances to awakening and revival. Like I said earlier, if we are afraid to address the hard things, how can we see change? We can't. So I'll dive right in.

From the time I entered New York I can tell you the leaders I met were giving it their all. But some were so desperate they did not know what they were doing, (as far as personal agendas). Others knew exactly what they were doing, and I can only hope repentance will grace them like a tidal wave!

One very influential leader so manipulated the circumstances around me that it nearly took me out of the game. This one was so insecure and afraid of loosing status with the people that measures untold were taken. Things about my schedule were presented to others as if this person was running the show. I was even told I couldn't do apostolic work in New York unless I went through this individual. I was being intimidated behind the scenes and when I tried to expose it, it backfired. I didn't catch on to what was happening until it was too late. This character was trying to increase their ministry off of my favor with the people. (Unfortunately, my naïve nature has always proved quite the vice in a world of hidden agendas.)

Now concerning specific hindrances, some were leading from a place of unhealed emotions. When this happens it is catastrophic for *all* involved. It opens the door to false doctrines and religious spirits. It also breeds territorialism, which is rampant in the church right now. All of these things combined, absolutely extinguish the fire of God. It puts the focus on what makes the man or woman of God secure in their leadership position, rather than the gospel of Christ. The gospel should never focus on what pleases man! This is heresy at its finest. Clearly, I experienced these manifestations in my presence, and whenever they cropped up, they did hinder the fire.

Now, there were several leaders who did not honor me at all, and really, my identity was mocked. A big problem was my gender; this is where most of the disdain originated. Women just don't receive the respect that men do. One leader wanted me to drive two hours so they could give me a word, publicly. This individual said it had to be done in a *certain way,* and refused to give me the prophetic word unless I submitted to their plan. God told me not go. He said this one was trying to place themselves over me in the spirit, which was a form of witchcraft. Then, in one meeting, a man grabbed the microphone straight from my hand while I was speaking! Crazy agendas, fueled by insecurity and control.

Now, there were also many places I stayed throughout my journey. One was quite astonishing. At the onset, I had in impression I was supposed to be elsewhere, but I stayed anyway. Before lodging, the Lord whispered to be careful not to end up like Evan Roberts. The voice was so small I brushed it off. I thought I was being paranoid because of all the other manipulation swirling around me. But no sooner had I forgotten it- I received an email. It was from a random person in another state warning me of the woes of Evan Roberts. Interesting. Then shortly thereafter was a phone call with someone else across the country. They brought up the same caution. Be careful not to end up like Evan Roberts. Hmm, strike three. A little strange.

Soon my body was increasing physical symptoms; and fear was wrapping me like an Anaconda. My money was gone and there was no one to call. I was eating less and less food and my trusty SUV was mostly, parked! Demonic spider webs were being woven; I saw a black widow in the spirit. So I stayed isolated, but grew extremely faint. I recognized the Spirit of Death, so I called my spiritual mom in desperation. She said a spider web was cocooning me, and every bit of life was being sucked out. This confirmed what I was seeing but nothing changed. In a short amount of time, it matured to the point that one morning I could barely swallow food.

Then that same day, one final call came in! Within two minutes the topic of conversation was you guessed it: Evan Roberts. (And I did not induce the theme!) Next came a word of knowledge that physical illness was verbally being projected upon me. I was shocked and admitted it was true. But I could not get my body to stop manifesting the symptoms. It took this former Marine to get the job done,

"Traace, you're going to have to gut it out and leave, regardless of how you feel. It's the atmosphere around you."

I was so weak I could barely lift my arms. I remained in bed listening through my ear buds, as this individual started praying in tongues. Within a few minutes I was able to pray too. Then after ten more, I was strong enough to stand and take my stuff to the car. Thankfully a benevolent soul gave some money, which enabled me to leave. I drove out of the driveway in a mix of panic and relief.

I was thirty minutes down the road when my car started making a loud racket. Then I pulled into a store lot to grab some food, and as my car was idling, it died! I prayed, and when it started back up, I took to the highway. But still, I could hear the rackety sound so I stopped again. I walked around my SUV several times, inspecting it and commanding it to function properly. I didn't have another problem. I will never forget some of these traumatic experiences and the lessons I learned from them.

NO MORE RELATIONSHIP

Now this chapter would not be complete unless I included: the family problems! Right before I left for Toledo my closet family member decided to end their relationship with me. I felt a tinge in my heart but the Lord gave me peace. This wasn't to say I didn't battle fear, because it was very real knowing there was no one to call if I needed help, or if I was in a bind financially. At any rate, I had to move forward. I wish I could say this was the end of the emotional trials that week, but here's what happened next.

I was scheduled to go back home to Oklahoma after Toledo. This would be my first visit since being in New York and I desperately needed to go to the house where my belongings were stored. I wanted to grab some summer clothes and do a little re-organizing. But no sooner was I roused with anticipation, than I discovered a relative was arriving that same weekend. Not good! This person always had a King Saul/David relationship with me, so I avoided interaction as much as possible. To make matters worse, the familial one was scheduled to stay in the room where my things were stored. This meant I would not be able to retrieve my summer clothes or downsize the load in my SUV. I was so frustrated. But I stayed calm, there had to be reason.

After finding this out, I called the one family member who had never betrayed me. I begged them not to reveal anything about my trip to the soon-coming visitor. (I wanted no words of jealousy or manipulation against me. I couldn't handle anymore emotional warfare.) But there was only partial compliance, it seemed blood relation carried more weight than God's ordination. I cried so hard after this phone call. I felt betrayed again, and even more alone. There was no one left to rely on. Then within a few minutes, I was dealing with another challenging call. It centered on some religious mentalities I had confronted openly in one of the cities. I put my own pain aside, in order to make some wise decisions and give proper council. It wasn't exactly a bed of roses, either.

As I was dealing with these issues, I was standing by a field outside of a car shop in the very hot sun, communicating back and forth with a mechanic. My compressor was out in my old SUV. We were trying to figure out the problem and which route was needed to repair it. What an afternoon! I managed to close out all conversations in the spirit of love, but my heart was utterly broken. I felt numb and had no time to process the upheaval with my family. It would soon take its toll. Now more than ever, I wished I had a best friend, or a loving husband to wrap his arms around me. Not so, I was completely by myself. I had to press on, and practice what I preached.

All of these things, and much, much more were whirling around me, while God was asking me to release revival and contend for a nation. I literally stood alone with Him, facing a people I had never met in a land I had never known. It was the toughest assignment I've ever done.

8

MAY 13TH

40 HOURS AFTER WELLSVILLE: Now the Wellsville school ended on a bright sunny afternoon and I returned to the yellow lake house. I had 40 hours to rest before driving west for Toledo. That night I had a dream about my revivalist friend. He was standing tall, and behind him was a huge mountain range. I knew the mountains represented spiritual warfare. So when I rose in the morning, I was still caught heavenly realms. I began to pray about what I seen and heard in the dream. I was swept into the most severe travail I had experienced for an individual, to date! The Lord showed me this man's calling was significant. I saw two mantles, one like Billy Graham and the other like Charles Finney. So I wailed and wailed through tears, because America needed revivalists to bring her to her knees in repentance. This brother in the Lord *had* to emerge on the scene!

I arrived in Ohio late the next night and this time it was warm. I had been anticipating this particular day to see if it would confirm another dream I had in January, while I was staying in Buffalo.

The dream: *I had seen the date "May 13th" while my revival friend from Toledo was standing right in front of me. A huge pane of* *glass was between us and he was taping a poster to the window. The poster was a picture of a worship band dressed in bright, vibrant colors. I knew it meant he was bringing a new worship into his city. After that, there was a great shift in his life and he was launched into a new season. That was the end.*

When I walked into the coffee shop to meet him, I forgot about the May 13th dream. But in the course of the conversation, I looked over to my right and saw a huge pane of glass! Just beyond it was a wall of vibrant colors. It jolted my memory. I proceeded to tell him the dream but I'm not sure he understood my lame explanation. Nevertheless, I knew it was a significant moment and an ordained time to be in Toledo. Soon, the coffee shop closed and we left. The next day I would speak at this man's fiery, young-adult group. I couldn't wait! Many friends from my first visit would be there and it would be good to see them again.

THE RIVER CHAT

16 HOURS LATER: Before the meeting that night, my revival friend and I decided to walk by the river. We sat in the sun; chatting about the message God had given me. Our conversation grew heated quickly, but we were working through some core issues. I had much to say about awakening in the church and the ways God had shown me to join in the task. He didn't agree and was resolute. I sat there calmly, thinking. Then right when I was about to say some harsh things, my mind flashed to the intense travail, two days prior. Then the Lord spoke, "He's just as called as you are Tracey!" He told me not to wound with my words.

This man, too was called to awaken the church in America. God wanted me to support that however it looked. So I axed my verbal negativity. And while we remained at an impasse, my quick-thinking friend suggested we go for food. So we headed back to the car. After a few moments of silence, the Holy Spirit spoke to him and he gave me permission to loose the fire the way God had shown me. I was a little shocked and somewhat apprehensive, but we agreed, and then hugged it out.

A few hours later, the evening service began with prayer before the worship. My fiery friend grabbed the microphone and loosed some juice like I haven't heard in a while! Others prayed too. I noticed for the first time I did not have to contend for the atmosphere over a meeting. It was already set. And it was fierce! It seemed my friend and the musicians were walking at a very high spiritual level. It felt like the top of the building had been blown right off! It was a wide-open heaven. As I peered into the city, it too was powerfully affected by these young warriors' prayers.

When the musicians began to worship, intercession was thick in the atmosphere, and my friend dropped to his knees near me. I couldn't hear a word, as the songs were loud, but I could feel a spiritual force coming from him. It was literally pulling me to the floor, as travail churned in my spirit for a move of God. Every time this man knelt to pray, the same force hit me. It was a deep passion and brokenness. I believe it was the purity of his heart and the fervency in his prayers that produced such tangible results.

The message I spoke that night was compelling, and since I was speaking before some incredible warriors, I cut them no slack. I presented the call for the nation of America, and spoke on the history of prayer in the earth from the past five hundred years. I talked of those who saw entire nations and generations changed for the glory of God. Some of these warriors were Evan Roberts, Charles Finney, Martin Luther, and John Knox.

KNOX

In my studies, I discovered the prayers of John Knox were undeniable. Bloody Queen Mary of England was a Christian killer during his lifetime. It is said she feared Knox's prayers more than the armies of Europe. That's a lot of prayer power coming from one person! Who says a tyrannous government has the last say? Even the highest office in a land must acknowledge the one who has the ear of Him Who created life.

ROBERTS

Then there was a young man by the name of Evan Roberts who lived at the turn of the 20th century. He was a powerful travailing intercessor. He gave his whole life in prayer for his nation to be born again, and he saw it with his own eyes! Not only did he see it, but he was the one God used to facilitate it.

Early in his life, God asked him if he could believe for 100,000 souls, at the time that was the entirety of his nation. Evan responded to God with action! He prayed, and he prayed in tongues. Once the reviving began amongst the people, it took three years for his country of Whales to be born-again. It is said the bars closed, and even the jails were empty, because no one was committing crimes. Now that's fruit! His passion for God impacted the whole planet. Even the one writing this book had her first fiery encounters for revival while reading about his life. One man's prayers in secret changed the globe. They are still changing the earth today.

FINNEY

As if Evan's life isn't enough to invoke a penetrating cry for holiness, Charles Finney is one whose legacy will live on for as long as there is human life in America. One does not need to excel in rocket-science to see the shift he brought to the Christian culture of his day. The supposed believers of his time were lukewarm, and a sorry example of the righteousness of God. Finney called them out! And he called them out to their faces. He looked the congregants in their eyes and demanded a response to the God they claimed to serve. In the end, they were faced with the reality that they indeed needed the Lord. Multitudes wailed in repentance in city after city, at the sinful state of their own souls. Even the vilest skeptics were converted. None could stand under the holiness God was releasing through Finney's words.

Finney paid a price. He gave his life. He traveled the state of New York while severely sick; even at death's door, but he continued with his mission. He traveled through snow and bitter cold, driving a horse and buggy. He relinquished threats on his life, and terrible persecution from other ministry leaders. He never backed down. He saw the birth of the second great awakening in America; he facilitated it. He was one man!

It is said the fruit of his revivals was permanent, as eighty percent or more of his converts remained faithful to the Lord. He adored the people. He would stay with them in New York among their own communities, loving them. I can tell you from personal experience his legacy lives on, because New Yorkers still speak of the man. They know where he was and what followed his steps. Finney was a man of holiness, fire and passion, and it forever seared a nation. The day I stood on his grave, the Lord allowed me to feel that passion. I felt the fire for America, and for souls. Prayers live on, and they remain eternally tangible for generations to come.

LUTHER

Last, but not least is Martin Luther. This man stood in the midst of terrible religious tyranny and deception. He not only changed his nation but he changed the course of history. He had the audacity to preach the truths of scriptures and confront the giants in the land with only a pen. You see the rulers of his day were oppressing the poor by misrepresenting God. He clearly articulated truth; line upon line, head-butting the demonic lies purported by those church leaders. Like Finney and Roberts, Luther, too, gave his life for the mission of truth.

As a friend of mine studied the great reformers, including Luther and she said, "Tracey, they all prayed in tongues. It was an emphasis for them."

GREATEST PRAYER MEETING EVER

The greatest corporate prayer meeting in all of history came after Jesus' death, burial, resurrection and His final ascension to heaven. It changed everything and empowered a few men to turn the known world upside down! The bottom-line revelation wasn't merely that all these people prayed and changed societies, nations and generations; it was *how* they prayed. These people were fervent, they were passionate and they gave their all. The bible is clear when it is says the fervent prayer of the righteous makes tremendous power available!

THE HISTORY OF AMERICA

After recounting these stories of utter transformation we must ask ourselves, what will be said concerning the history of prayer in America? Will it be said we risked it all, or we feared to pray in tongues with power? Will it be said we gave it everything, or we held back because of man's opinion? Will it be said we loved not our lives unto death, or that we feared the Socialistic government? Will fear of the church hierarchy system paralyze us, or will we live everyday as a martyr? And finally, will we find ourselves written in the history of a nation born in a day?

THE OKLAHOMA WEDDING

Two days after I spoke in Toledo, I left for Oklahoma. This would be the wedding of all weddings. He was nearly my best friend and a spiritual, big brother. She was a prayer companion and full of fire! It was a dream come true of sorts for me to see my brother, married. He had been there for me when no one else was, he took me in when I was homeless, gave me money when I was hungry and fixed my car when it was broken.

He had been through more pain than just about anyone I had met. The injustice was unbelievable, and he never complained. I had prayed much for God to bring him a wife and restore his life. Now this monumental day had arrived and I was a witness with my own eyes! The day after the wedding, I left for central Arkansas.

CENTRAL ARKANSAS

24 HOURS LATER: One of the worst tornados in history touched down in Moore, Oklahoma, just as I left the northeastern part of the state. Four hours later, I arrived safely in Arkansas. There was

a twenty-four hour worship event scheduled around my coming. It was good to just sit in the Presence of the Lord. These people were like family to me. After the worship weekend, I spoke on Sunday morning at the host church. I gave the reports of all that had happened in New York since I left. We had a lovely time. It ended all too soon and I drove back to New York. I was headed to the Canadian border, near Vermont.

9

NORTHEN AND EASTERN
NEW YORK

AKWASANSE PRAYER SCHOOL

78 HOURS LATER: And twenty-four hours of driving, I made it to the Canadian border. Akwesasne! The Mohawk's turf. This was one of the highlights of my trip. Not only am I part Native, but also I had a dream about this people hours before I received the invitation to come. Here's what happened. It was an early morning in April, 4 a.m. to be exact. The dream was clear.

I was driving into a city at midnight. I proceeded slowly and with much caution, as there were gigantic buffalo (larger than my vehicle) lying on the sidewalks. Their legs were tucked up nicely beneath them and they were almost pre-historic in size. I knew if just one decided to stand up and walk toward me, my car could be crushed. I was in awe and slightly terrified.

Then I awoke to a text message, "Akwesasne, May 31-June 2."

I knew the interpretation! The buffalo represented the Native Americans. They were sitting on their laurels and God was sending me to tell them to stand up! They were the most powerful leaders in our land and they needed to rise. This was their nation; they were the host people. I couldn't wait to tell them, I was so excited. On a side note, the cover of my first book sported an image of myself in Native war paint. In 2010, the Lord showed me I would be significant in helping Native American's gain back their voice. So I boldly published the Indian-themed book cover. During that time period, I wept and wept for the people to arise.

As I arrived for dinner, I was greeted by the typical question,

"How old are you?"

I smiled and giggled on the inside. The dinner was great and it felt like home. Soon we were off to the church. That night when I started teaching, it was the heaviest warfare since I arrived in New York. It was familiar in the spirit realm because it felt like Oklahoma. The intensity was crushing me but I kept hurling light out of my mouth. By night two the atmosphere seemed a little better, but nothing significant, yet.

Then the third meeting was a Sunday morning, and as I taught, I watched light shatter the atmosphere of the sanctuary! It was glorious. After the final teaching, I called everyone to the front to speak in tongues and be anointed with oil. But the pastor's long time friend stayed seated. He couldn't speak in tongues and felt he could not participate. He had been seeking the baptism of the Holy Spirit for years, but to no avail. Then the wise pastor told him to walk forward! On the way up the aisle, the man spontaneously started speaking in tongues. He wept and wept. It was beautiful and his face glowed for a long time.

Afterwards, the pastor's wife asked how they as a congregation were going to move forward, now. I suggested we do seven nights of intercession, a different place every night. Many people would come and experience the change together; then all would shift. We agreed, and it was done!

7 DAYS ABLAZE FOR AWKESASNE

24 HOURS LATER: The next evening was night one of the intercession. I was blown away by the beginning moments! I sat down on the first row, while the people sat behind me in the congregation. We were all facing forward. Then, I grabbed the microphone and struck my drum. We began to pray in tongues and a force of authority exploded from the attendees. It brought me to tears. So I turned around, expecting to see a huge amount of people. They were few in number. I focused back on intercession, trying not to crumple from the power exuding out of their spirits. I thought, we've tapped the mother load!

After a short bit, I handed over the microphone to the Mohawk pastor. He was fervent in tongues. I realized I handed it up in the spirit. He prayed and prayed while I warred on my drum. He then passed the lead to a young man who was also Mohawk. He too was fervently speaking in tongues. I was amazed at his authority. I continued drumming and singing songs of triumph, while his words "settled the issue" in the atmosphere of the region. He went on and on in his heavenly language, as the pastor approached the altar and sat beside his native drum. He began to play along with my little drum. It was awesome; the sounds, the praises to God, all demonstrated the mystery of His might. The buffalo were standing as the entire room engaged!

The next several nights we utilized other church's sanctuaries for the two hours of intercession. Each time a different group joined us. Many people came out, and they were hungry for God! Not all the places were Mohawk, either.

MOIRA

The city was twenty miles from the Mohawk reservation. The structure was old and once upon a time had been a train station. After that, it became a bar. Currently, it was a church filled with dark wooden beams that revealed the uniqueness of both origins. We started the two hours of intercession as normal, with an explanation of the vision and why we were praying in this specific manner. I took a seat before the microphone and starting speaking in tongues, while the congregants behind me joined in. It didn't take long to realize the atmosphere was insubordinate; there was a heaviness that could not be shattered.

I was perplexed, and then remembered the scripture I had mulled over all day. It was half of Colossians, chapter one. I simply read it out loud over the territory. That's all it took. Suddenly, everything became warm with the tangible Presence of God! I saw firsthand the power of His written word to settle the issue. This night was phenomenal, and I will never forget it.

NORWOOD

This city was about twenty-five miles from the reservation and the church was on a main road. When I arrived, I found it small and packed-out. The pastor was a white man. It would be interesting to see how those attending would merge together! Looking back, it was an awesome experience. We prayed in tongues for the first thirty minutes or so, but I noticed something different. From the onset, there was light and a tangible glory all around us. God was drawing me to stop speaking in tongues and sing only, while I continued on my drum.

I gave way, and found myself in a strong prophetic flow proclaiming the promises of God through spontaneous songs. This went on and on. The congregation was strong behind me. I declared through worship for the great gifts within the people of Norwood to arise. I could see into the future as I was singing, I literally watched the changes happen in the spirit realm. The results would be: the prophets would now prophesy, and "that which had been withheld would no long be withheld".

As I sang, I continued to marvel; just since last night, the heaviness was gone, and a veil had been ripped off. I could see it clearly, but was at a loss for the explanation. But the Lord solved my mental quandary.

"It's because the Mohawk pastor staked the land today in a sixty mile radius. The veil over the region has been removed. You do not need to fight anymore, just worship, for the breakthrough has come."

So I did! The prophetic flow continued. I remained in a trance-like vision, mostly unaware of those in the room. I could see directly into the hearts of men and women throughout the entire region. I knew their gifts from small to great. I announced over them, as if they were standing right before me. I sang and sang the words of God, and was deliberate with every beat of my drum. I was pounding His words into the ground and calling out over the people. At the end, I looked behind my seat at the Mohawk pastor. He leaned up a shared what was happening in the spirit realm.

As I was playing my drum an angel appeared. It was dancing and dancing, whirling in circles across the altar in front of me. After taking a double-look, the pastor realized it was not an angel, but it was Jesus. He was dressed in full, bright white regalia! He was dancing over the cities of the region, and every time I hit the drum with my hand, fire sprang up from a city. Jesus was dancing over the land as I praised Him on the drum! The rudder was steering.

SUNDAY MORNING #2

On the day before I left, I shared the word God had given me for the powerful Mohawk people. I revealed the buffalo dream, and then told them to stand up! I commissioned them with the phrase God spoke in my ear, as I entered their territory one-week prior,

"The host people of the land are to host My Presence."

I told them a story from the bible. The true account revealed the fact there are repercussions in a region when God's Presence is at hand. Here's the skinny: the Philistines had stolen the Ark of the Covenant from Israel and brought into the house of Dagon, their idol. When they set it next to the statue, the following morning they found the idol on its face before the ark of God. So Dagon was perch back up. But the next morning it was discovered again,

Dagon had fallen on its face before the ark. This time, its head and hands were severed off.

The story continues…The Philistine region was struck with mice and heavy destruction. Tumors and painful boils appeared on the people. So they sent the ark of God to another city. The same thing happened in that place! So for the third time, the ark of God was sent to a different location under Philistine control. But on this occasion before it came, the people cried out; they didn't want to meet death! Finally, the ark of God was restored to Israel.

The moral of the story for this context is God's Presence causes physical changes to a city and a region. (I was not implying there would be negative repercussions, but simply stating territorial change comes from the Presence of God.) The Mohawks were to host God's Presence which would bring a powerful, godly change to their region.

ROAD BLOCK

24 HOURS LATER: As I left the Mohawk territory, I traveled a beautiful country thruway beside a river separating Canada from America. (On the way in the first time, I almost drove out of the country by accident, but I stopped for directions. That's when the border patrol pointed me to this side-road and told me to take the "hidden highway".) This was the path I was traveling when suddenly; I noticed the two-lane, rural road was blocked. Five soldiers were standing in the street and had stopped the car in front of me. When it drove away I opened my door, as my window was stuck up. Two soldiers walked to my driver's side, and three to the passenger's side.

"Where are you coming from?" one asked, into my open door.

"The Mohawk reservation." I replied.

"Are you alone?" hurled the next question.

"Yes, just me and my stuff." I thought, I couldn't fit anyone else in this car! The first man proceeded to let me go, but the other man was angry. He hurled more questions, as he tightened his jaw, over and over.

"What were you doing there?" he asked firmly.

"Prayer meetings." I looked him straight in the face.

"Oh. I'm just asking!" he said. "What religion are you? Just curious!"

"Christian," I shot back.

The first man questioning me grew rather nervous and wanted me to be released.

"Who were you with?" came another personal question. I answered him.

"Do you know such and such?" he asked.

I said, "No."

"Why do you have a sticker that says Texas?" He asked.

(There was a half-peeled inspection sticker from 2010 still on the glass.) "Because I lived there." I said.

Finally, I shifted the conversation. "Is everything okay? What's going on?"

"Yes, this is routine. You may go," the angry man said.

I thought this is anything but routine. The car in front of me was greeted with smiles and waved through in mere moments. I wondered what the three soldiers were doing on the passenger side while I was being questioned. Either way, it was very unnerving. An attractive woman traveling alone, stuck in an odd predicament like that, not the most comforting. The surroundings were so rural anything could have happened. I pressed on, and stopped at the first gas station for a coffee. When I got back on the road, the ever-familiar sound of prop planes grew louder and louder. Something was wrong with my (at least) 250,000 mile SUV. I had four more hours to go before I reached my next destination, and in my spirit I knew it was a severe issue. I comforted myself by pondering a lunch meeting I had in Arkansas, two weeks prior. The powerful warrior woman looked up from across the table with a pointed index finger.

Through a firm voice she stated, "And Satan, I bind you from your plans against her car. Hands off! You cannot touch her car!"

So I let the proclamation strengthen my faith. There was nothing I could do anyway, I had to teach an intercessory meeting at 7 p.m. Obviously, I made it safely, but just in time. That week the mechanic said I was very close to my driver's side, front wheel erupting into flames while driving!

LAKEVILLE

4 HOURS LATER: I arrived at a little school in the middle of nowhere. It was surrounded by green, rolling hills and tall silos. The scenery looked like a portrait from the Sound of Music. The meeting place was in one of the classrooms, where a group of lady intercessors awaited me. What hearts of love these women possessed! I shared the vision for New York and the rudder message for America. They were greatly encouraged. Then I played my drum for a bit as we prayed. I was out of steam from all the driving and intense nights of intercession, so they decided to pray for me. They prayed off the beaten path, asking God to send me a godly husband to accompany me in my travels. I couldn't agree more! I left the school and stayed in a hotel that night.

14 HOURS LATER: I departed from my hotel and drove twenty minutes to the Grand Canyon of the East. It was a several, mile long park. I went through half of it, stopping at certain spots to look at the amazing valleys. The place was very rural, wooded and isolated, and since my car was making odd noises, I opted to leave

before it broke down. From the there it was an hour drive to Geneva and that's where I would sleep for the next several days. The following morning I went to Utica, New York for a 10 a.m. meeting. It was a two hour commute.

LEADERS IN UTICA

14 HOURS LATER: I arrived at a minister's meeting in downtown Utica. Afterwards, a prayer school was scheduled for three weeks out. It would be trailed by seven nights of intercession. I returned that afternoon to Geneva and settled into the Boston-style home I had visited a few months prior. It looked like a setting right out of Italy, too. Outside, a round street curved in front of the dozen or so, three-story houses. There was a huge fountain in the center, and on the other side of that fountain was the main road, which was also lined by Boston-style homes. Beyond that, and a few more feet, was lake Geneva. This valley of water was huge, deep and very blue. My view sat slightly higher in altitude, making it easy to see. It felt like a paradise, and I wished someone had been present to enjoy it with me.

That evening I decided to go for a walk to see the beauty of the flowers and the unique neighborhoods. I went by a few quaint shops and a tiny, hilly cemetery that reminded me of Ireland. Then I expired for the night. Inside, prophetic murals layered the walls of the large home. One section really stands out to me. (I had noticed it at the meeting back in March.) It was solid black with a huge, white stallion leaping straight out of it! In the background the terrain was dark and mountainous, while behind the peeks a red hue was visible. There was a stormy feel to it and the first time I saw it, it nearly took my breath away. It looked like a scenario right out of my first book; The Tale of a Screaming Heart, which is a prophetic allegory about America and intercession.

It seemed I was living out this tale on my one-year journey. I penned it a few years prior, but now I was observing people, structures and cities that were within the pages. (So, I actually wrote about them before I encountered them.) My mind escaped to that portion of my book.

...The room had completely vanished. In its place was a white stallion. A young woman dressed in battle armament was upon the back of this majestic creature. Her hair was long and flowing amidst the blustering wind. She was gripping the horse's mane with her left hand, while wielding a sword in her right. The blade was massive, and polished silver in color. Nothing but pitch-blackness surrounded vision. The horse and its warrior were combating a gigantic, dark force. Hooves were ferociously beating the wind and the sword was slinging toward the beast. The thing was huge and seemed to over match the animal and its rider, nevertheless, the two drove it back.

...After the black entity retreated across a vast amount of territory, the stallion lowered his head to the earth. The Young Woman slid off its back, quickly thrusting her sword into the ground, claiming victory... It seemed one day, an intense battle would rage for the country's very existence. But a female warrior would arise, riding upon the strength of her generation to defeat the advancing, evil combine.

What a prophetic picture of warrior-heart praying to reclaim a nation! Not to mention it was another confirmation that my every step was God-ordained.

THE ESTHER ROOM

That night I slept on the third story and opened the window overlooking the fountain. It was 80 degrees, so the breeze was pleasant. I could hear the water splashing and the echoing bells of the gorgeous, old church next door. When I plopped down on the bed, I looked up and noticed another mural. This one was of Queen Esther. She was extending her scepter across an unmeasured territory. As I fell asleep, I marveled at the places God was sending me.

BERNE PRAYER SCHOOL

48 HOURS LATER: I embarked upon a rather interesting drive to Berne. It was three hours from Geneva so I gave myself extra time

to find a hotel before the prayer school started that evening. As I drove, I discovered the roads were flooded throughout the Mohawk valley. (They were rural and two-lanes, running through the midst of hills.) While driving these curvy roads, emergency alerts kept popping up on my phone. "If I checked the local news I would know which areas to avoid." Unfortunately, I had no home in which to check the local news, and the radio stations said nothing. I didn't know which roads to avoid, I had never driven them and there were many miles to go.

I decided to stop by a filling station along the way and ask which routes typically flooded and which ones were safe, and then I made a mental mark. I checked my GPS often and when I saw a road that was mentioned, I took a different route. But my phone signal was spotty, frustrating the journey even more. So I called the ministry a few times for help, but no one replied. As usual, I was on my own.

By this time, I only had a short window to find a safe course, a hotel, and then eat dinner. The minutes were being eaten up by frequent stops, as well as wrong turns. I discovered people were losing their homes, because the hotels in the towns were all booked. Finally I found one; thirty minutes from the church. This was great, the first session started in half an hour. So I checked into the hotel and flew out of the parking lot, but could not shake the weakness in my body. I needed nutritious food, and fast. (I had left at lunchtime, planning to find a restaurant when I arrived, but the hubbub caused me to skip lunch, and now dinner). Sadly, the gas station nearby would have to do!

At this point, it was still possible to make it on time, until I hit a roadblock. So I hurriedly parked my car and ran across the road to the other side of the bridge, where the firemen were standing. (I'm sure I looked crazy running in my 4-inch wedges.) I told them where I was headed, and then asked which way was passable. Fortunately, I did not have to re-route. I arrived at the meeting ten minutes late and was quickly introduced to the pastor, as I passed by him in the hall. I was hungry, exhausted and had to teach for the next two hours. I could barely think. So after they handed me the microphone, I took out my drum and began to sing to Jesus. The glory came and strengthened my body, and then I proceeded with the rest of the night.

On my way out, I asked if there were any fast food places nearby, as the obvious rural layout proved there were no restaurants. I was told there was a gas station right by my hotel. I remembered the word God gave me about giving up my comforts. (Now, the host church offered a house for me to stay in, but other people were there, and I needed to gain my strength back through seclusion.)

I was so thankful for a bed in solitude that night, but the next morning came early, as I raided the one lone, gas station. Three rice protein bars, one half gallon of milk, an orange juice and probably a candy bar! I taught six hours that day and afterwards anointed every one with oil, praying in tongues over them. The Presence of God was very strong as many could not stand during the impartation. This prayer school was awesome. Lots of people came from all over the region, as it was right outside of Albany, the state capitol. The struggles of floods, gas station food and full hotels were worth all it! I finished early that evening and ventured out a ways down the main highway. I found another filling station, this one had chicken salad sandwiches! I was a happy camper and drove back to my lodging. The next morning would again, come too early. I had an hour drive before I spoke in another city at 9:30 a.m.

CATSKILL

16 HOURS LATER: I started the trip to a beautiful church in Catskill! It was slow going this Sunday morning as my body ached for sleep and my spirit for refreshing. I followed my GPS to the mark, but it put me on the wrong side of the river. So now, I would be late another time! If only I had the strength to get up earlier, I would have done it. Honestly, I was doing good just to make it.

As I entered the room full of people, I sensed fire. I had no time to prepare anything. I walked nearly straight to the pulpit and exhorted them for an hour. I told them they were called to help bring awakening to America. We must position ourselves to be in agreement with God, I explained. A massive wave of repentance is needed and we can birth it through our intercession. The people were riveted and greatly encouraged. Much emotion was stirred upon hearing how God sent me to them, they were important in His plan for America. The commission was the same here as in every city. Gather the intercessors and pray! Pray in tongues and worship the One Who is worthy. Be the answer. No more pointing fingers at those who needed to "do it right" within Christian communities. It was time for us to be the rudder.

MINISTRY SCHOOL IN ALBANY

19 HOURS LATER: It was Monday evening, the day after Catskill. I had been invited to a ministry school to teach for three hours. I told them I would probably leave prematurely, because I had an early morning meeting the next day in another city. Not to worry, they were just thankful I could come! This was such a blessing to me. It was an unusual meeting, in the sense that these were young people. Ninety percent of those I had been working with were over the age of sixty. These were in their early twenties, at best.

I taught for about an hour and half and had nothing more in me. So I left and drove down the street to grab a hotel. I was looking forward to a good night's sleep. On the way, I stopped for a hot coffee to sooth me. As I entered the lodging lobby there was a middle-eastern man at the desk. I asked him if there were any rooms; he had one left. After a few more questions, he hesitantly offered a different one. So I took the better of the two. The conversation at the counter was humorous, as he was trying to explain why their hotel was worth the price.

My reply went something like, "I don't eat imitation eggs, I refuse to consume pork and I don't swim in toxic, chlorinated pools."

While we were talking, a very matter-of-fact older man came in from the street with a clipboard. He was asking questions about cameras and how long the information was stored. The clerk was nervous. I just listened. The odd inquiries rolled on and on, as the man taking the survey seemed legit and very pure. Then another employee of the hotel showed up. He was way too friendly with me but I joked around with him, not too concerned. I blew off the commotion and went to my room. I could finally relax. It was just before 10 p.m. Then it happened. I spotted the camera in the bathroom. That's why they acted different about this room! Ugh. I had no time for this!

My mind raced over some of the personal questions the "too friendly" man had asked me. I thought of the clipboard person. I thought of the rampant, human trafficking. I looked at the second door in my room. Then I was scared. I was a pretty woman alone and I was being watched. Quickly, I texted someone for advice; there was no response until the next morning. I couldn't think of anyone to call for help in this city, it was in the heart of Albany, New York. I felt strongly to leave, so I packed my things and headed to the front desk. The clerk was acting peculiar and inquiring. The Lord told me to play dumb, like an air-headed woman, since they had all of my personal information. I left with the reason that I should have picked a hotel closer to my morning meeting.

I loaded my stuff in the SUV, and then sat in the parking lot, looking at the cold food I had not had time to eat. Now it was 11 p.m. I had no place to go. I started to cry from utter exhaustion. I was so tired I couldn't think of what I should do. But after a release of tears and some prayer, I remembered the hotel I stayed in the night before. It was over an hour away, but they always had rooms and it was safe. So I drove, shaken up and super sleepy, but I made it. Finally I was able to fall asleep at 2 a.m. The next morning came early as I had a meeting at 10 a.m. in another city, nearly an hour away.

THE UNSPOKEN CITY

7 HOURS LATER: I walked into the little room of a nice church to see a group of intercessors waiting and praying. I shook off the scariness from the night before and entered right into the atmosphere. I taught for about an hour when they wanted to pray.

126

As we spoke in tongues, intercession fell in the room. People were on their faces. The atmosphere turned intense! Then after a while, the leader of the group announced that what I taught would be their new way of doing things. The leadership was making the shift from dry prayers to fiery ones; this was what they had always wanted!

Immediately, someone started asking questions. A strong traditional spirit was prevalent in the tone. They wanted to focus on personal prayer requests and had no desire for the meetings to shift into intercession. A rather heated argument broke out among the group and I was caught in the middle. The person was strongly opposing me and the revelations I was bringing. This went on for thirty minutes. I stood up and walked out, pacing the hall and playing with my iphone. The voices rattled on back in the room. I didn't have time for this mess. I was so tired of religious spirits!

At the end, the leader blessed and honored me. Many of the attendees also, thanked me for coming. That night I dreamed an alligator was attacking me. I knew what it meant. I was thankful I was safe in the tower of the Lord and the person's words against me could not prevail. At least this one was only a crocodile. The last time it was meat-eating dinosaurs! It's sad that we have horrendous atrocities happening across the earth, from people being tortured and murdered for their faith, to human trafficking, not to mention all kinds of abuse and poverty. And then people like this person want to attack the very power of God. Unbelievable. Selfishness is a vice.

A few weeks later, I received an invitation to return to do a prayer school, but only for their group of intercessors. It appeared no effort would be given toward inviting others outside of their own congregation. Inevitably, this was a self-focused mentality. It also exposed their lack of ability to perceive my spiritual labor. The commission God had given me was not to strengthen the individual church approach. It was to mobilize God's people in cities and entire regions to birth repentance. They all needed to shift together, not just one church. Only those with humble and contrite hearts could receive this grassroots vision of awakening America through united intercession. Obviously, I declined the invitation. Even though I liked the leader, I wasn't interested in fortifying man-made structures.

WESTBROOKEVILLE

8 DAYS LATER: I had just come off of a break, but it was not nearly enough. My body was so depleted from the intense journey that by this point, I needed a year to sleep. Not to mention the last eight days I spent in a moldy house without air-conditioning. I was thankful for a bed, but my lungs wheezed the entire duration. Now it was time for me to drive an hour to another church. Once again, I blazed through the winding, mountainous roads of rural New York, right into the gravel parking lot of a packed out church. The leader who invited me was opening up with some revelation about prophetic signs in the earth.

When it came time for me to speak, I shared the mission and the vision God had unraveled about New York. There was an emphasis placed on the different realms we live in as human spirits. I told them the first dimension was the earth realm and God's dimension was His spirit. We had to position ourselves in God's realm where all the miracles remained. Our bodies were merely conduits for His power. We could access whatever is in His sphere by allowing our spirit to dwell there and soak it up. Then it's a simple transfer, making miracles visible!

The pastors of this congregation were so hungry for God. Revival cloaked them and they didn't even know it. I left that night around 10 p.m. I found a hotel not too far away in another rural town. I stayed there two nights, and then headed for Massachusetts.

10

MASSACHUSETTS

39 HOURS LATER: I departed for Massachusetts. It was quite a haul too, but I was ready and very peaceful. After driving all afternoon, I entered the region and noticed beautiful mountains on both sides of the highway. But there was also a dark smog through and through. I grew extremely sleepy for about fifteen minutes, and then it lifted. This was the city that boasted 2,300 witches and I thought, "You're not getting one inch! Nasty witchcraft."

I couldn't help thinking about my first book, again. The heroin in the novel was a female Native American warrior who traveled through portals, (or her prayer closet) to the northern most part of her nation to deal with core strongholds. One of them was witchcraft, which I suspected to be this Massachusetts city. (Another was a "crescent dome" and that ended up being Toledo.) I know you're probably thinking, who writes this stuff! Ha-ha!

DINNER

After I arrived at my hotel, I met the man from Massachusetts and his wife for dinner. She was so sweet and he was very honoring of me. I was thankful. They made me feel comfortable. After dinner we went to church for the first night of the prayer school. I taught and it was good. I was surprised there was no warfare against me. I slept well that night, and the next morning was a beautiful day. I left the amazing Inn viewing lots of sunshine, and then I found a nice, hot coffee.

When I drove through the curvy entrance of the church I could see the main spirit over the entire organization. It was definitely one of religious nature and I knew this would call for the war drum! So, shortly after we began the first session, I grabbed my djembe. I played a commanding rhythm not only over that place, but also over the entire region. The people joined me instantly by praying in tongues. They were quite fervent too. I was surprised, because I had done very little teaching and had not anointed anyone with oil yet. I sang songs of God's glory and power. There was tremendous authority and I could sense a spiritual shift taking place in the land. I was cognitive of the wells from the first great awaking.

I finished teaching the prayer school and concluded about 4 p.m. The leader told me afterwards that when I started playing my drum they slipped into a zone. It was intercession! On my way out, I commented to him that I had not experienced the intense warfare expected from the area witches. His reply, "They didn't even know you were here. You came in and out so fast they didn't have a chance to communicate about you."

UTICA PRAYER SCHOOL

22 HOURS LATER: I left Massachusetts and drove 3 hours in the afternoon to Utica to teach the first night of the prayer school. I arrived to a packed out inner city, African American church. And boy, was it hot outside! There was no air conditioning and New York was experiencing record breaking temperatures. It's a good thing I was used to Oklahoma. If we had been there, most of the people would have been in heat exhaustion. This was a long night; it was three and a half hours of teaching. Most who attended this first evening were not intercessors; they were congregational members. Whenever that happened the teaching always took an evangelistic flare. God considered those in the room, high priority. It was hard ground but the people were hungry. I could sense a lot

of them struggled with worldly desires, which meant they were prime for revival!

The pastor of this church was amazing and so was his house prophet. They knew God! The thing I enjoyed most about this school was the passion of the people. Their words of fire interjected during my teaching only stirred me up more. The next night was also a three hour teaching, followed by a time of impartation with anointing oil. I prayed over several leaders and it was a very effective time.

These two days would be followed by 7 nights of intercession. I couldn't wait; the nights of prayer were my favorite times. If I could have done nothing but play my drum and pray in tongues the entire trip, I would have been the happiest person alive! But I spent most of my time teaching and imparting. This particular school was strategic in the fact that the house prophet had been given a vision to interact with the civil authorities in her city. This female powerhouse also had a heart for the streets. She was mobilizing the people to prayer-walk the highways and byways. This is where the strategy came in! My school was to help equip them to undertake this task.

7 DAYS ABLAZE FOR UTICA

NEW HARTFORD 24 HOURS LATER: Now, the nights of intercession for the Utica region were super fiery. Quite a few came out too. This first night we met in an old Catholic convent. The room was packed and the heat was still on, so we sweated our way through! I will never forget this night. We prayed in tongues for a good hour and a half, I was playing my drum the entire time. Then the last thirty minutes, I shifted and hit a flow of worship. I went into the zone, vaguely aware of the people around me. The Holy Spirit brought to my mind something He had shown me earlier in the day.

It had been raining in the Mohawk Valley, and in Utica the downpours were atrocious. (You could barely see to drive in the city during the daytime; that's how hard it rained.) I sensed a spiritual connection to the weather and clearly saw fast-flowing water washing the crops right off the fields. I knew if breakthrough didn't come the floods would devastate the land. So I continued to sing spontaneous songs to the Lord while my spirit scanned the northeast coast. Then a phrase hit my mind; over and over I sang it,

"The name of the Lord, the name of the Lord."

As I watched and sang, I saw a very tall wall forming in the atmosphere over northeastern America. It was a shield. The Lord was creating a buffer as I sang! As soon as I hit the last drumbeat and ended for the night, the Lord spoke, "The rain has stopped."

I knew the flooding was over, but when I exited the building I still wondered if I would see rain. But there was none, and the downpours never came back!

Now, the way I set up these nights of intercession, everyone prayed in tongues at the same time. It was up to Holy Spirit to navigate each individual in prayer. This night, I was focused on a regional level singing to stop the floods, but that didn't mean everyone else was on the same topic. As matter of fact, no one knew I was singing to stop the rain, nor did I know the theme of their intercession. I could have asked, but we prayed right up until the placed closed and the doors were locked.

WATERVILLE

24 HOURS LATER: The second night, we met at a larger church in another town. There were quite a few in attendance, most of which had not been to the school. The pastor was a pillar in the spirit. He was solid and unmoved by trivial issues. This night was probably the hardest night of intercession on my entire trip. I think because I was late arriving, and did not have a chance to explain to the new ones the format and commissioning. (The first few moments of every intercession time were crucial, as my information was literal equipping before we prayed.) I'm not saying we weren't effective because I'm sure each one grew personally. I just wished we could have tapped higher realms.

UTICA (THE INNER CITY)

48 HOURS LATER: The fourth night we met at a small church in downtown Utica. Very few attended. I walked in carrying my drum and wearing jeans. I was introduced to a finely dressed pastor, who looked me up and down. She was rather smug.

Her vibes were strongly, "Who does she think she is?"

By now I was used to this crap. I ignored her and walked to front of the church and sat down behind the microphone. I did my typical few minutes of "information equipping", and then I shut my eyes and commenced to pray in tongues. I played my drum and settled within myself to intercede as if I were the only one present. I released God's glory on the streets out front, because it wasn't such a nice neighborhood. I interceded for drug addicts, those in sexual addictions, gun violence and the like. I believed with all my heart I was planting seeds that would one day crop up in revival!

The Lord revealed a funny thing to me this night. You see; *He* needed my words in these various places. And if the only way this could happen was by setting up prayer meetings for me to lead, then so be it. My authoritative intercession was enough to bring change to the region! Knowing this revelation made it easy for me to disregard the critics. Plus I knew this was the same spirit Jesus dealt with in Israel. The Jews thought He should come as a violent, conquering king, but He came in a manger. He was meek and lowly. Humility is an instant rock of offense to the prideful, which care more about outward appearances, than the condition of the heart. God encouraged me many times on my journey that He was using me to expose the motives of people. Many were choosing His ways of prayer and humility, but some were roused to anger at my presence.

At first, I was afraid to hurt or offend them, but He convinced me to let the divide happen. He said the regional leaders needed to see who was really on the side of the Lord and who was not. They needed to be aware of the vipers in their midst. That's why so much conflict surfaced, and I had to become acclimated to God's ways. Any approval of man left in me was burned up for sure! God was serious about cleaning the rudder.

ONEIDA

24 HOURS LATER: The fifth night of intercession was off the beaten path. We gathered in a large barn on the backside of a house in a neighborhood. It was the coolest setting; concrete floors, a loft and beams! We arranged our chairs in a circle and commenced to pray in tongues. We prayed for nearly an hour when the Lord said to stop. This had never happened before, (I mean, I had stopped meetings because people were not with me, but this was different.) I leaned over to the house prophet of the host church and inquired of her. She sensed the same thing. So we paused. I began conversing with the people.

Soon stories emerged of defilement on the land and high statistics of immorality among the population. Also, they relayed an account of a socialistic commune that had been established nearby in the nineteen sixties. Horrible mayhem happened and such uncleanness. After quite a few minutes, the stories kept rolling and I had heard enough. There was darkness all around now, (as a result of rehearsing the evil) and we were in a pit, spiritually speaking. I thought to myself, how do we get out of this? (Nugget: intercession is only effective from a high place.)

So I hit my drum, the room echoed. I released another deep, thud. I was trying to penetrate the darkness in ground and shatter the atmosphere. Neither changed, the hole was deep. I kept playing the djembe but no one joined in. I thought, this is the time to do what the Lord sent me to do! I started singing and lost myself in the spirit of prayer. I battled with my spontaneous songs and rhythms of power. After about five minutes I sensed a crack of light in the atmosphere. Then ten minutes, the ground was shifting. I kept going. For thirty minutes I sang songs of high, high praise. (Declaring directly to God Who He was in the earth and all of heaven.) This was the only thing that could cleanse the land and the atmosphere. Finally, the people linked in, and their voices rose.

The last few minutes the glory grew so thick no one could speak. We sat in silence. And nothing was moving in the spirit realm, because nothing was left! It was as if every dark thing, stronghold and curse just vanished. I opened my eyes and could barely see, because I had gone so deep spiritually. We all sat staring at each other. Then at once, we loaded into our cars and parted ways, victorious.

UTICA (THE INNER CITY)

24 HOURS LATER: Finally, the last night of intercession was upon us for Utica. We were back at the host church and I was looking forward to it! The people filed in and we began to pray, but I noticed a woman on the second row, glaring at me. She had one bad attitude. She did not like my drum, my expression or me. I ignored her for the first thirty minutes but every time I opened my eyes, I saw her. Eventually, I went to the house prophet about it. (I learned the lady was a major leader in their church.) But she gave me permission to address everyone. So, I did. In the most diplomatic way, I explained we could not move forward in prayer if we were not in unity.

"There are those in this room who do not like me. I just want to explain, this is voluntary…"

Before I could finish, the fiery, female prophet shouted from the side of the sanctuary, "What she sayin' is, if you don't like it you can leave!" I chimed in, "Yes, please leave."

So the bad attitude woman left, along with another lady. We marched onward! We prayed a great victory and the fiery prophet joined me over the microphone, while I drummed and sang. Power hit that place and sealed the deal in the atmosphere for Utica, New York.

11

THE CITY

LONG ISLAND

4 DAYS LATER: Since I was anxious and did not want to be late for this meeting, I split the drive into two days. After a night in a hotel, I set out on a Friday afternoon toward the city. I did pretty well until I hit major traffic and a plethora of interchanges. That's when I saw the sign! It read, "tunnel". I quickly changed about four lanes and exited the highway. I found a side street and halted my car. I did not want to get stuck in a tunnel! (My A.C. was going out and my driver's side window was stuck up, not to mention my SUV was black. I was concerned about being trapped in record-heat temps in NYC traffic with no airflow.)

As soon as I stopped, I grabbed my phone to check the map. There was a text from someone in Utica. Oh, that's right, he's from Long Island! He used to live in New York City. I quickly called him and rattled off my location and asked for his advice. He was very calm and assured me I had already passed by the tunnels, "But if you find yourself in one, then bless God, plead the blood of Jesus and drive through."

Then I realized how silly I sounded. Finally, I made it to Long Island. The people were lovely and I was staying in the home of a Jewish pastor and his wife. I felt honored! The first night we worshiped, and then the group discussed the state of prayer on the Island. I learned a lot. Since I was accustomed to teaching about prayer, it was good for me to hear the condition of hearts and different opinions.

12 HOURS LATER: The next morning I woke up feeling very weak. I had caught a virus and wanted to crawl back into bed, but I was scheduled to teach at 10 a.m. I pressed through and taught for an hour and a half on bible stories, spotlighting intimacy with God as the only way to save a people.

KING DAVID

King David was an amazing demonstration of intimacy. His continual gaze upon the Lord, while playing his instrument, caused him to learn God's character in the most remarkable way. The result: David knew God personally. This is what gave him the faith and confidence to stand before Israel's enemy, Goliath. David had the power to take out this giant because of his relationship with the Lord, and for no other reason. The rest of Israel believed in the same God as David, but the difference was David actually knew Him. Anyone could have hurled a rock at Goliath, but only God could drop him. David's power was in the Presence He carried!

So concerning Long Island, there were many strongholds and "Goliaths" taunting. The revelation was simple; throwing rocks at iniquitous strongholds will never destroy giants. They only fall by those who know God. (Or stated another way: God, neither demonic strongholds are moved by human status or Christian liturgy.) The message: focus on one thing, knowing God and loving Him. This, in and of itself, would cause evil to fall because individuals would start conducting their lives differently. This would induce a ripple effect of healing the sick, delivering the oppressed and winning souls- God's strategy for taking a nation. This is enacting the first commandment followed by the second.

TABERNACLE

The Tabernacle was an amazing prophetic picture for those who intercede for mankind. In the Torah it was set up in three segments, the outer court, the inner court and the holy of holies. The inner chamber of the holy of holies was where the High Priest offered supplication on behalf of the people. He did not stand in the outer court or the inner court when He went before God. Similarly, intercession cannot remain "surface level" and truly change a nation! Just as only one could go behind the veil, effective intercession always comes from the most transparent place with God. The heart for a nation to be born-again can only come from the secret place. It cannot be manufactured or learned from church or bible school, the Spirit of God must *impart* it.

ESTHER WAS MARRIED

Even Esther had to be married to the king in order to plead for a people! We must be joined to the Lord in the inner chamber of our soul if we are going to change a city or a nation. Too many pray from a place of head knowledge, or from liturgy. Learning is not bad, but we cannot sincerely know a thing without experience. If it is merely something we know in theory, how can we know it will stand up under the test? This is one reason why so many supplications are prayed with very little results. Theory praying is for the birds!

True intercession comes from a deep, deep understanding of the will and emotions of God. What are *His* original intentions? Those who are audacious enough to discover the Creator's original purposes first-hand will be blessed enough to see His redemption. Deliverance comes no other way but through Jesus Christ, the Son of God; the One Who redeemed all mankind and Earth itself. The mystery of God is found in knowing Him! After this teaching we all loaded up and went for pizza. It was awesome, and I was happily refueled for the afternoon session.

AFTERNOON TEACHING

The afternoon segment was quite unique. As I started sharing about God's call on New Yorkers, the people were not engaging. They were very distracted, and my words were not reaching them. So I scanned the audience. And there it sat, a dark fog hovering above their heads. The evil spirit had entered with them and was preventing engagement at the heart level. This entity wasn't merely a hindrance in the room, but also the prevalent, evil spirit on the entire Island. It had gained its corporate home through a specific attitude in God's people, which was "acts of righteousness are far more important than knowing God". Hence, the reason for the subject matters in the first session!

Before expounding on what I was seeing, I decided to address the people personally. I asked if it was hard for them to concentrate. The unanimous response was yes. So rather than continuing to *teach* on intimacy, God told me to *demonstrate* intimacy.

He said, "Just worship Me. You, Tracey, sing to Me."

So I stopped talking and picked up my drum. I sang to the beautiful Lord for thirty minutes instead of following the schedule to teach. At first, people were not worshipping. Even ministry leaders held back. (Administrators often think they are exempt because the service is "for the congregation". But Christianity is not about hierarchies or performances.)

Finally, I yelled out to the people in the midst of my singing, "I am not performing."

Most joined in, some still refused. Then the afternoon portion ended. We were supposed to be done for the day but the Presence of God was rather strong, so I was asked to continue. We had to move out of the sanctuary into a back room because of some pre-arranged repairs. During the transition a worship leader said he felt the ground shake while I was playing my drum. The pronouncement of God's kingdom was undeniable!

In the back, everyone packed into the little room like sardines. I taught for two more hours. They were now sponges, soaking up the impartation of authoritative intercession. How hungry they were for the deeper things of God! During both sessions many were present from other countries. Especially dear to my heart were the Chinese! They were busy interpreting my message for those in the room who could not understand English. For some reason, this really moved me.

I received an email from one of the women, who said, "What you teach is really, impartation."

She got it! Her English may have been spotty, but in the Spirit there is no language barrier.

THE TOUR

Before I left the Island the host pastors took me on a tour. We passed by a historical site for Wycliffe bible translators; I took several pictures! Next we went by a beautiful beach. And soon we were driving by the Russian embassy. It was very plain with two nominal gates. The grounds were covered with a bunch of overgrown bushes and grass. I couldn't see any buildings and I was informed, no...bo...dy stops when they pass by. It was an eerie feeling, as I tried not to stare. Along the way, a story was relayed by my host about a United Nations meeting he attended. The people were very dishonoring because he was Jewish.

I sat silent in the backseat. I was shocked, and hearing the recollection made my heart hurt. I loved Israel and the Jewish people. They were God's firstborn. The Messiah came through the Jews and God had blessed the whole earth through them. They had been keeping feasts, or God's preset appointments for thousands of years. To me, this made them pretty special! Not just any people would commit to following God's strict orders for so long. But they were paving a way for mankind to understand God. So now we have the fulfillment of prophecy through Yeshua Ha-Mashiach (Jesus the Messiah).

I have to say, in a world where anti-Semitism is rampant and Christians have adopted replacement theology; it is utter stupidity to ignore our roots. God is the one Who picked the Hebrews/Jewish race. God is the One Who asked them to keep His feasts, or set times. God knew what He was doing. God has a way of operating in which the mind of man cannot understand, unless Holy Spirit enlightens it.

By now you know I have a passion like none other to see America revived. But *greater* than that passion is my love for Israel to show forth the praises of God! As long as there is breath in my lungs and tears in my eyes I will cry out for the land God calls His own. Nothing anyone can do or say will remove His favor from Jerusalem. That city was created to mirror His great city in heaven; it's in the foundation. And no ruler, president or earthly king can remove it. It belongs to the God.

BACK IN UTICA

16 HOURS LATER: I left Long Island early the next morning and was still fighting a fever. I arrived several hours later back in Utica to stay at a host home. There was no air conditioning in my room and New York was still experiencing quite a heat wave. My fever elevated and my electrolytes plummeted, so I rested for five days but grew no better. No matter how much I slept, strength evaded me. Honestly, I think my body was crashing from the extensive journey.

I decided to meet a friend for coffee in spite of my struggles. I thought venturing out might help. I had given so much to others; I had no time for fellowship. This day I spent an extended time in conversation on the deeper things of God. My friend's spirit was strong and impartation came into my soul. We met again, and I grew stronger still! At the end of our time together, I was prayed over. God's glory transcended the atmosphere around us. I was thankful for people who paid a price to consecrate themselves, the fruit is always evident. I had been depleted to the point that I feared for my life, although I told no one. But after the prayer, I was on the upswing.

12

THE TRANSITION

SYRACUSE AGLOW

6 DAYS AFTER LONG ISLAND: This was a one-time meeting on a Saturday morning. I drove an hour and was greeted by the Presence of the Lord as I walked into the small sanctuary. It was beautiful and so were the people. Mostly ladies were in attendance. After the amazing worship, a woman took the microphone and shared the biblical story of the widow giving two mites.

"She only had two mites, but she gave all she had!" The words echoed in the room and ricocheted in my mind.

I heard nothing more of her message because Holy Spirit started talking to me, "You are like the widow woman. You gave all you had, which was your life. It was all you possessed but look at it now."

My forty years flashed before me! I saw nothing but abuse, betrayal, injustice and sickness. I had nothing to offer God but a life full of suffering. All else had been taken, but that's all He needed. He received it, blessed it and then multiplied it. The Lord then said, "Share your testimony." Nervousness hit like an arrow. I had never publicly shared my life-story. Most of my friends didn't even know the entirety. I had no choice but to be obedient. In my mind I faced the battle of being rejected, yet again. But I stood up and went to the front of the room. Out came my words over the microphone,

"Many of you know who I am and why I came to New York. You have attended the prayer schools and experienced the fiery intercession. Today, I will share my testimony for the first time, publicly."

Then I spoke for probably forty-five minutes. I shared the bottom-line details of the malfunction in which I was surrounded by day and night, until adulthood. From the age of fourteen on, much of my time was spent crying and crying alone my room, while staring out a window. (I was counting the years until I could be released from the oppressive environment.) I told them I had been severely rejected, treated harshly and surrounded by injustice; induced even by family members.

The yearlong physical and verbal abuse from my teacher at school, began at age five. All of my life I was tormented by my peers and never accepted. Then when I became a follower of Jesus, it wasn't long before Christian leaders, who either used my gift for self-promotion, or made sure I would never rise to triumph, reduced me to nothing. Adding insult to injury, I had been criticized, hated and severely abused by most of the men in my life. Other people I trusted said I would never accomplish anything and no one would ever want to marry me. There were so many verbal finalities enforcing my worthlessness! Also, more than once, I had survived the brush of death in my body.

The faces seemed a little shocked but they listened, intensely. Then, I concluded the end of my personal life and gave a fiery commission for our nation! My final statement was meant to provoke them to do the impossible in the face of atrocities: I told them injustice had continued in my life until not too long ago. And

I was alone, homeless, jobless and without any support, "…But I am before you sane, and giving all glory to a good, good God! He has raised me up to help bring a mighty awakening to this nation. Everywhere I go people are restored and set on fire for the Lord."

I told them God made a warrior out of me and He could do the same for every woman in that room! It didn't matter what people said or did, if God owned you, you could conquer the world. I really encouraged the ladies to achieve huge tasks and accomplish their dreams. After I finished, the leader was amazing; she rose, and just stood next to me. Other women surrounded me. I asked if I could play my drum and sing to Jesus. They were more than happy. I sat on the front row and drummed with an authority given only by God.

Many joined me in singing and there was much strength in the room. Some were on their faces in intercession. It was a powerful moment. Then they began to prophesy words of remuneration over me, and they set money on my drum. I was shocked. My worries eased of how I was going to survive alone. This was further proof God was going to take care of me. Afterwards, one of the pastors commented how the fear of the Lord was on that moment.

BATH PRAYER SCHOOL, NUMERO DOS

6 DAYS LATER: I returned to Bath, ready to rest! A regional leader opened her home to me and said God had told her I was wiped out. So I was fed tons of wheatgrass and given the use of a hammock in the sun. I laid on it for several days. I tried not to engage, but she was a talkative lady and my efforts were somewhat thwarted. After a week of rest, I did a second prayer school Bath. This was a good school, as the hungry came back and new faces graced the meetings. The anointing at the end was remarkable. The fear of the Lord was very weighty, and the impartation went deep!

Afterwards, the most incredible thing happened for me personally. I had been praying for a place to stay alone, so I could recover from the pull of the people. Also, I needed to write this book. So a lady in attendance offered an empty duplex for two and half months! This was such an answer to my heart. For the first two weeks of my stay I barely saw sunlight. It was so refreshing to come and go as I pleased without interruptions or questions. Every day was sunny, and 75. Mountains and a beautiful market place nearby surrounded me.

While I was here I experienced a financial miracle. It was an early morning when I went for coffee. And since I only had a small amount in my bank, (reserved for car insurance) I pulled the last twenty-dollar bill out of my purse. My words trailed the zip of my bag, "I trust You Lord."

Then roughly an hour later, I received a phone call from a married couple. Someone had given them money to pass on to me. So I received gifts cards for gas and the awesome grocery store across the street! This amount provided all of my food and fuel for two months, it even covered some car repairs. I was so thankful.

WELLSVILLE PRAYER SCHOOL, NUMERO DOS

3 WEEKS LATER: This was the second prayer school for the people of Wellsville. The very mature attended and it was effective. I was winding down my yearlong mission. I could feel the transition breathing down my neck. This would be my last prayer school until my new season…or so I thought.

AUBURN

12 WEEKS LATER: I had sensed for several weeks Auburn was supposed to host a prayer school. But insurmountable odds kept arising; so breaking into this city would not come easy. Now, God had connected me with a mobilizing intercessor, as well as a worshiper who understood what God was doing apostolically. So these two searched out churches to host the weekend event. It took a while to find one willing to consider the notion, but finally a prospect arose! Then, the all too familiar question emerged, "Who's your covering?" I preferred to speak to the inquiring pastor myself on this matter. So after a few days of missing calls, we connected over the phone.

The conversation barely began when the man bottom-lined me,

"Who's your covering?"

My first thought, "I know he is going to reject the request because I don't believe in 'coverings'."

My second thought, "This means I only have one shot to impart the vision for awakening in America!"

Also, I wanted him to know what was happening across the rest of the state. So I proceeded to give the information as concisely as possible, but he wasn't too interested. He just wanted to know the tell-all-question. Finally, I said to him in a diplomatic way I didn't play the game of coverings. The conversation ended quickly, and I soon received a report the church-board declined to host the prayer school. Now, the two people with whom I was working would have to find another location. This took a while, but God chose Auburn! Eventually another place opened up, but they weren't sure how many would attend. I knew the pattern would be the same as many other cities across New York. God would give the increase, and it would be more than a few!

Two weeks before this prayer school, I grew sick with a fever. The place of solitude had mold in the basement and when the heater was turned on my lungs paid the price! So in the midst of sickness, I had to pack my things and move to another city. I made quite a bit of trips in the cold and this made matters much worse. Finally, I settled into a new place while a severe infection had settled into my body.

After a few days of rest, it was time for the weekend prayer school in Auburn. I had to drive ill for two hours, through snowy, narrow roads. Argh! But on the way, my spirit felt the wind of revival, specifically the Finney heritage. It was stronger in this region than any other city I had visited in the burned-out district. And the Lord whispered to me: history is changed by the few. He said those present in the Auburn prayer school were enough to birth a change to sweep their city. I knew if they gave attention to this revelation they would see great salvations in the community! When I pulled in front of the church, I was pleased to see its location in the middle of a downtown triangle of commerce. The parking lot adjoined the police station, while a few bars and diners surrounded it. It was a walking-distance, bustling community.

I spoke that night for a couple of hours on intercession. I encouraged them that a small group of people could change history. I also emphasized what it meant to have the heart of a warrior. It was well received. Even the pastor who denied hosting the event was present. He approached me afterwards and sheepishly explained it was not his fault I was prohibited, it was a decision by the board. I told him no worries; I was where God wanted me!

15 HOURS LATER: We decided to do a noontime prayer in the sanctuary of the host church. I was looking forward to it, as the Lord had put this time slot on my heart, months ago. It would be the first time of doing a lunchtime event. When I arrived a few minutes after twelve, prayer was already in motion. So I sat on the front row, and prepared to play my drum to provide an atmosphere for them to go deep in intercession, but no one was praying in tongues. I asked for a microphone and proceeded to lead out. I assumed it would be rough because I hadn't taught much yet. And I had missed the opening moments for "equipping". I was right.

Nevertheless, we endured forty-five minutes, at which time I opened my eyes and glanced down a few seats on the front row. A man was staring straight at me. He had moved near me at some point and I could tell he was agitated. So I saluted him, and then I stood up to close the meeting. He interrupted me, and was clearly out of order. I told him his questions should be addressed another time by a pastor or leader in the area. Then the Lord showed me he was drunk.

So I halted everything and asked him, "Who invited you here?"

He was vague and mumbled around, trying to avoid the answer.

Again, I re-worded the question, "Who do you know in this room? Anybody?"

"No." he finally stated.

I refused to move on, and told him he was important to God. Long story short, he walked in off the street, and that day, he drank for the first time in five years. He had been in prison for killing two people and had gone through a recent separation with someone he loved. He was not a Christian- or even close. At this juncture, a pastor present invited the man into the hallway where they could talk privately. Another man in the congregation who came to pray, joined them. The rest of us decided to back up our friends with some spontaneous worship and intercession. This time our prayer was much easier; another forty-five minutes flew by, when I stopped singing to go pay my meter. As I looked out the window, I could see police cars had pulled to the front of diner across the street.

"We're stirring stuff up." A leader spoke, as I passed by.

I opened the sanctuary door and two more discomfited people whizzed by. Electricity was in the air due to our fiery prayers and it wasn't over yet. I came back from paying the meter, and continued drumming and singing over the microphone. All prayed along fervently. At this stage, it was nearly 3 p.m. We could have continued the rest of the day but I was exhausted from sickness and playing the heavy instrument, so we ended. The man who had entered was now sober and smiling. He thanked me for reaching out to him. (He gave his life to the Lord that day and continued attending the church, until he moved away!)

3 HOURS LATER: It was time for night two of the prayer school. As I entered the church I saw it was packed-out. I was happy to see a few young faces too. They may have been twenty, at best. The teaching began and the people were pulling strong on my spirit. After the three hours, I called everyone to the front and anointed them with oil. I asked one of the young people to come to the altar and play my drum. The whole group was praying in tongues and

the atmosphere was tangibly charged with God. Then everyone tapered off and returned to their seats. They remained engaged, but not as intensely as myself. I could not stop speaking in tongues. I continued over the microphone for a while; with no music or drums. I could see all of Auburn in my spirit, I was crying out over the land and people. Before long, I opened my eyes and trailed the regional leader from Ithaca, as he came to the front.

He said, "I have a word for Auburn."

He spoke for five minutes on what he had seen in the spirit over Auburn, and for the people. As he finished, two pastors gathered over to the side and whispered to each other. In response to the word, they decided to have two nights of worship on the coming weekend. I was elated! These were pastors and one was from another church. God was unifying His people and igniting intercession. Even though the Finney well was being uncapped, this would have to be a movement of God's people in Auburn, not just one man. Nash's intercession was still alive and well, and so was the fear of the Lord that emblazoned Finney. So if the citizens of Auburn would stay the course, they could carry the torch and ignite this generation.

THE HEART ATTACK

A week or so after the prayer school for Auburn, I received an email. It read as follows:

"Monday morning my husband had a heart attack. He fell to the ground and was white and cold, and did not respond. I called out to him. Because we had just attended your prayer school, I automatically leaned over him and prayed in tongues. It took much longer than it should have for the ambulance to come, because they couldn't find our house. Then it was a half an hour drive to the hospital. A main artery was ninety-five percent clogged, and he was having an attack all that time. They put in two stents, and no further surgery was required. There is no damage to the heart. He is now home again. My husband told me, that while he lay there lifeless, and unconscious, he could hear me praying in tongues. He is convinced that is why he made it to the hospital alive." A year later, the man is still doing well.

TESTIMONIES AND A STORY

The pastor of the church who hosted the prayer school relayed one unbeliever came to the school out of desperation, because of an upcoming court date. She had been arrested for a DWI. She had never experienced speaking in tongues and she came to both services. The woman loved it and she has never been the same. The pastors believed she experienced deliverance with the praying in tongues. This church also has had amazing testimonies of healing and financial breakthrough. They've had an increase of prayer. The members from their church that came to the school have seen the importance of prayer, tongues and worship for life, growth and revival!

13

THE ORACLE AND
THE APOSTOLIC HUBS

I suppose you are wondering how all of this turned out; the scores of cities and leaders, and the multitudes of intercessors who partook in my one-year journey. The conclusion I must say is one for the history books, or shall I say, one where history repeated itself. As my twelve months came to a close, I was walking through my place of solitude when I discovered a book on a shelf by Charles Finney. (Holy Spirit Revivals by Charles Finney).

I picked it up and flipped ferociously through the chapters. I was captivated as I read his stories, told in his words. The cities he had visited were the same ones I visited. Tears streaked my face, as I realized I was walking the trail he blazed. My heart was strengthened and justified, as he retold the persecutions from Christian leaders. I felt I was sitting down with a spiritual father.

His sentences warned of the challenges that accompany revivals in upstate New York. He told of the dangerous, snowy roads he endured to bring the fire of God. He told of the diagnosis of certain death as he coughed up blood, due to sickness and exhaustion. He pushed through it all, and kept traveling. Somehow, he made it into his eighties, bitterness-free and satisfied with the fruit of his labors.

A few of his recounts shook me to the core. They were stories of those who had rejected the Lord and died in the midst of the people. As they slipped into death they were screaming about the torments of hell. Finney's preaching was different than just a puppeteer from a pulpit. He cared about the people and would often ask each individual questions before he began his sermons.

In my opinion, this was one reason for his success; he answered the queries of the laity. He wasn't trying to build his ministry or look anointed. Further proof was the endless hours he spent in the homes with people. They had heard about his meetings and sought him out because the Lord's conviction rested over their communities. It was no secret why his converts remained true to God. They understood their commitment was a lifestyle and not just a confession.

As I pondered the extraordinary, heart-felt methods of Mr. Finney, I sat down the book and proceeded with my meal. My mind escaped to a heavenly realm, as I saw a leadership across New York answering the "questions of the people". It looked like a grass roots discipleship plan made up of several hub cities. The leaders in New York with which God had connected me had the apostolic authority to build His kingdom in their prospective regions. They were a new leadership of sorts that God was raising up. The prayer schools were simply the catalysts to uncap their abilities and call out of hiding those who would help them.

The Lord told me the cities in which I had held consecutive nights of intercession would be the hubs! This was quite a strategy, and I never saw it coming. I had simply had been following His instructions for a year, step by step.

FOREWARNING

Suddenly, the phone buzzed and it was the prophet from Ohio.

(The one from Chapter 3.) He was calling to ask if I would consider being part of a prayer team back in Toledo. I said yes, and then I took the occasion to tell him of the idea of the hubs in New York. He chuckled and reminded me he had prophesied that quite some time ago. Then before he hung up, he asked a question as prophets often do,

"Has God given you cities or the state?"

"Umm." I muffled.

He continued, "Because if God has given you the cities, then you will have to let the first one go. If He has given you the state, well then…"

"…You may have to let God just burn it with His fire. But we'll be here for you when it happens." The prophet's words rang out.

He went on to explain when Joshua took the promised land, they had to let Jericho go. The first city was an offering to the Lord. I knew the answer to the riddle and I didn't like it! God had given me the state. My heart sank. (I knew the outcome before I even started the task.) But a statewide meeting was called anyway. It was to inform the leaders of the apostolic vision that would sustain the work of the Lord and build a foundation for the next, great awakening. Many, many came, and I think the conclusion is best explained through a revelation in the nighttime.

THE SWORD AND JOAN OF ARC?

The night after the statewide meeting I had a dream…

"I was standing inside of a building near a window holding the Joan of Arc sword given to me. A masculine figure, much taller and broader than myself, appeared, and stuck a pistol to my temple. It was the size of my head and it resembled a round, futuristic atomic bomb. As I looked up at the character, I was confused because it kept shift-changing genders. (I knew it was a Jezebel spirit!)

155

As I pushed the gun slowly away from my temple, I said quietly,

'What...do...you...want?'

The person gasped loudly with their mouth wide open,

'Aha!'

And reached down and ripped my sword from my hand, running off so fast, I did not have time to respond. I looked out the window in haste and down into the streets, watching the person run to all the people with my sword. I looked back in my hand, and they had put their deadly pistol in it. This made me the guilty party because the gun was 'illegal'. So now I was framed for the being bad guy, when in fact, I did nothing. (I was the one being pistol-whipped!)

Immediately, I thought I should retrieve back my sword and dispose of the pistol before it could damage someone. The dream ended with me failing to retrieve my Joan of Arc sword, while the angels took away the gun, and then cleaned up the clutter."

Now it all made sense. At the beginning of the year the Lord spoke to me about Joan of Arc. He said she knew she was going to die before she died, but she chose to give her life anyway. I also knew the sword in this dream represented the one given to me when I was in Bradford, Pennsylvania.

"You remind me of Joan of Arc." The leader said. "I want you to have it. I've waited to give it to the right person and I feel like you are the one to have it. When Joan of Arc received the sword, it was a crucial time in her life."

I knew I was going to lose New York. I didn't want to face the reality but it was true. I had uncapped the wells and accomplished what God sent me to do. Now, my assignment was over. If I had pushed through the Jezebel attack it would have been disastrous, leading to many casualties. So I quietly rode off into the sunset knowing God is not mocked, and whatever a man sows, that shall he also reap. I had forsaken all and sown my life into those fields, and one day, I will grace the roaring mountains again. But until then, the key lies somewhere in the hand of time, waiting for only the pure in heart to grip its destiny.

Made in the USA
Coppell, TX
01 February 2025

45259363R30099